THE OREGON TRAIL

The Journey Across the Country from Lewis and Clark to the Transcontinental Railroad

WITH

25

PROJECTS

Karen Bush Gibson
Illustrated by Tom Casteel

~ More U.S. History titles in the *Build It Yourself* series ~

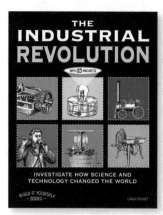

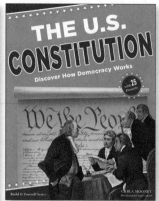
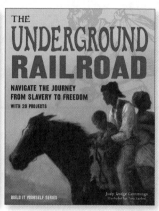

Check out more titles at www.nomadpress.net

Nomad Press
A division of Nomad Communications
10 9 8 7 6 5 4 3 2 1

This book was manufactured by Versa Press
East Peoria, Illinois
October 2017, Job #J17-07767

ISBN Softcover: 978-1-61930-576-2
ISBN Hardcover: 978-1-61930-572-4

Educational Consultant, Marla Conn

Questions regarding the ordering of this book should be addressed to
Nomad Press
2456 Christian St.
White River Junction, VT 05001
www.nomadpress.net

Printed in the United States.

CONTENTS

PS

Interested in Primary Sources?

Look for this icon. Use a smartphone or tablet app to scan the QR code and explore more! You can find a list of URLs on the Resources page. If the QR code doesn't work, try searching the Internet with the Keyword Prompts to find other helpful sources.

the Oregon Trail 🔎

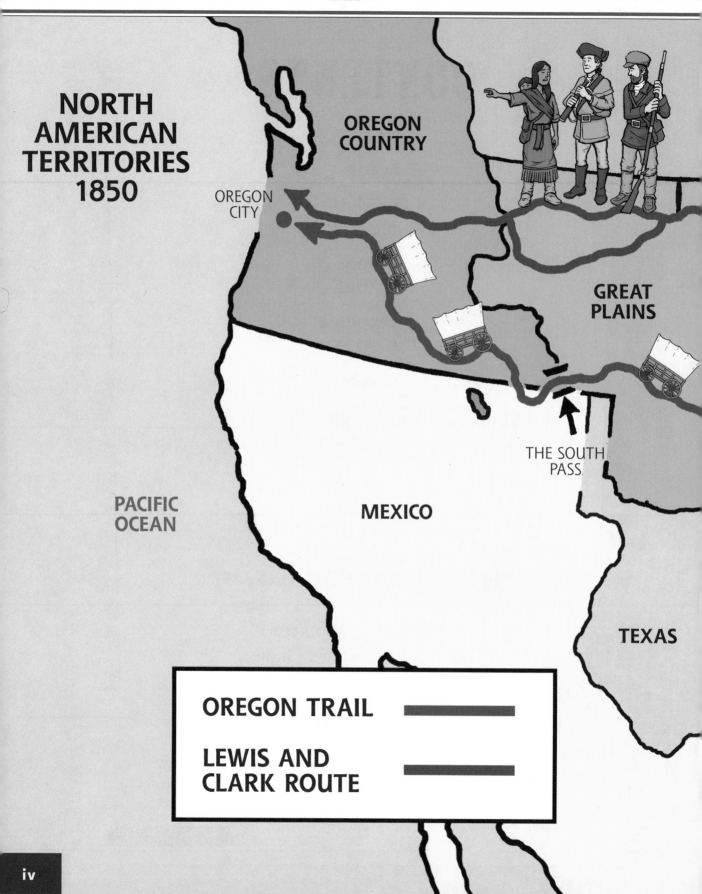

NORTH
AMERICAN
TERRITORIES
1850

OREGON
COUNTRY

OREGON
CITY

GREAT
PLAINS

THE SOUTH
PASS

PACIFIC
OCEAN

MEXICO

TEXAS

OREGON TRAIL

LEWIS AND
CLARK ROUTE

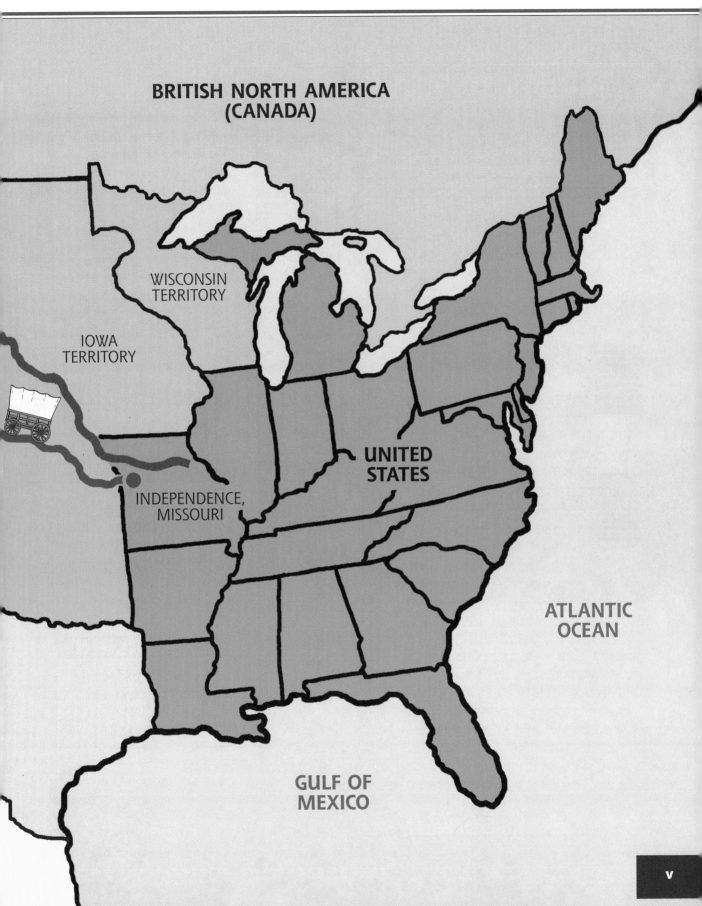

BRITISH NORTH AMERICA
(CANADA)

WISCONSIN
TERRITORY

IOWA
TERRITORY

UNITED
STATES

INDEPENDENCE,
MISSOURI

ATLANTIC
OCEAN

GULF OF
MEXICO

1793: Scottish fur trader Alexander MacKenzie becomes the first European to make an overland crossing of North America.

1811: Astor sends an overland expedition, headed by William Price Hunt, to Fort Astor. Their route from American Falls to Astoria will become part of the Oregon Trail.

1803: With the Louisiana Purchase, the United States buys the Louisiana Territory from France.

1812: Eastbound Astorians led by Robert Stuart discover the South Pass over the Continental Divide, but its location is not shared.

1804: The Corps of Discovery Lewis and Clark Expedition leaves on its journey to the Pacific Ocean on May 14.

1820: The Missouri Compromise is agreed on, admitting Missouri to the United States as a slave state. The compromise prohibits slavery in the remainder of the Louisiana Purchase north of Missouri's southern boundary.

1804: Lewis and Clark meet Sacagawea, who joins the expedition.

1805: The Lewis and Clark Expedition reaches the Pacific Coast.

1824: Jedediah Smith rediscovers the South Pass.

1810: John Jacob Astor establishes the Pacific Fur Company to explore the fur trade west of the Rocky Mountains. He sends the *Tonquin* to Oregon Country.

1836: The Whitman and Spalding missionaries, including the first white women to travel the Oregon Trail, successfully navigate the trail and establish missions in Oregon Country.

1811: The *Tonquin* arrives at the mouth of the Columbia River on March 22. Fort Astor, also known as Astoria, is established.

TIMELINE

1840: The Joel Walker family proves that children can travel pioneer trails.

1843: The first wagon completes the entire journey and the Great Migration on the Oregon Trail begins.

1846: The Donner Party is snowbound in the Sierra Nevada Mountains after following bad advice from a guidebook.

1848: Gold is discovered at Sutter's Mill in California.

1849: The California Gold Rush begins.

1850: The Donation Land Act is passed by Congress.

1860: Abraham Lincoln is elected president.

1860: The Utter wagon train is attacked by Indians. Eleven settlers and 25 Native Americans die.

1861: The Civil War begins on April 12 at Fort Sumter. The Southern states secede from the Union.

1862: The Homesteading Act is passed by Congress.

1862: President Lincoln signs the Pacific Railway Act.

1864: The Civil War ends and President Lincoln is assassinated.

May 1869: The Transcontinental Railroad is completed at Promontory Point, Utah.

1880: The last wagon train journey travels the Oregon Trail.

1883: The Northern Pacific Railway connects Chicago with Puget Sound in Washington.

1887: The Wounded Knee Massacre results in the deaths of more than 250 Native Americans, including a large number of children and women. Remaining Plains tribes are put on reservations.

1971: The Oregon Trail video game is created.

THE JOURNEY **BEGINS**

Imagine an America in which almost everyone lived in the eastern half of the country. Even in the early 1800s, when the population was much less than it is now, it would have been crowded! People living in the nineteenth century knew they'd have to do something to fix the problem of a growing population. They looked westward for a solution.

The **Oregon Trail** was part of this solution. People moving west needed a route to follow. The Oregon Trail was a pathway from Missouri to Oregon that people traveled in search of space, **fertile** farmland, gold, and a wilderness rich with **natural resources**. The Oregon Trail was the way to a better life.

Oregon Trail: the route settlers used to travel from Missouri to the West Coast during the 1840s and 1850s.

fertile: land that is good for growing crops.

natural resource: something from nature that people can use in some way, such as water, stone, and wood.

prospector: someone who explores an area for valuable natural resources, such as gold.

regulation: an official rule or law.

immigrant: a person who moves to a new country to settle there permanently.

crop: a plant grown for food and other uses.

persecution: to treat people cruelly or unfairly because of their membership in a social, racial, ethnic, or political group.

boundary: a line that marks a limit of an area, such as land owned by a country.

WORDS TO KNOW

Families, hunters, trappers, and **prospectors** set forth on the Oregon Trail. They went despite the many dangers and the risk of failure, or even death. Many embarked on the journey because their very survival depended on making the trek. Others went because of that streak in the human spirit that makes us walk toward untouched land, sail into unknown waters, and fly to the moon.

Take a walk through parts of the West today and you might still see wagon ruts in the land. They are left over from the steady stream of settlers who traveled from one side of the country to the other. These wagon ruts mark a period of time in the history of the United States that was both terrifying and thrilling for those who lived through it.

NINETEENTH-CENTURY AMERICA

When the United States greeted the 1800s, Americans had worked through many of the growing pains of a new country. New towns were springing up. People were forming state governments to provide a framework of **regulations** for the growing population.

And grow it did. Many **immigrants** came to American shores because the United States had the reputation of being the land of opportunity and a chance for a better life. People came looking for the chance to make money and support their families. Many were fleeing **crop** failure, rising taxes, or religious **persecution** in their countries.

The United States began to get crowded, and Americans moved into the wilderness of Kentucky, Tennessee, and Ohio.

The population still surged as people wanting new opportunities continued to arrive from other countries. Settlers moved as far west as the Mississippi River. On the other side was land as far as the eye could see. The few explorers and trappers who had crossed the Mississippi reported a place rich in fertile land and wildlife.

The War of 1812

The years after the American Revolution, which lasted from 1775 to 1783, were largely peaceful years, except for the War of 1812. This was a European war that spilled over into North America. On U.S. soil, the War of 1812 was largely a matter of **boundaries** and arguments about who owned what among the British, French, and Americans. Battles were fought both at the U.S.-Canadian border and in the American South. By 1815, the war had ended, and America concentrated on growth.

BIRTH OF THE OREGON TRAIL

The U.S. government, Americans, and people new to the country agreed—this land needed to be settled. But before people could start moving west and founding towns, the land had to be explored and a trail created.

President Thomas Jefferson ordered an **expedition** to be sent into the wilderness. From May 1804 to December 1805, Meriwether Lewis (1774–1809) and William Clark (1770–1838) led a team across the western half of the country. While the route they found was too difficult for the wagons that came later, they made the first maps of the area. The expedition provided valuable knowledge for the **intrepid** traders, hunters, and settlers who came later.

Other explorers followed Lewis and Clark and found alternate routes, including what would be named the Oregon Trail. During the early years, particularly from 1800 to the 1830s, it was mostly fur traders and early explorers making the trek by foot, horse, or boat. In the 1840s, settlers began using the Oregon Trail as a way to move west and settle new land.

For the next 40 years, a steady stream of people followed across prairies, mountains, deserts, and rivers. Some were intent on making money in new business ventures. Most were immigrants and settlers who followed in wagons filled with every belonging they owned, on their way to a new **homestead**. More than 400,000 people made the trip.

DID YOU KNOW?

People have been playing the Oregon Trail computer game for more than 40 years. Starting in Independence, Missouri, players purchase supplies and travel west, **negotiating** hazards and hunting for food along the trail. As on the actual Oregon Trail, disease and accidents are potential problems.

You can play a version of the game at this website.

play Oregon Trail 🔍

Harriet Scott Palmer

Harriet Scott (1841–1930) traveled from Illinois on the Oregon Trail with eight siblings and her parents in 1852. She was 11 years old. This is an excerpt from her memoir, *Crossing Over the Great Plains by Ox-Wagons.*

"August passed. We were nearing the Cascade Mountains. The oxen were worn out, and the wagons were in poor condition to cross' the mountains . . . Some wagons had to be left; some of the oxen were poisoned eating mountain laurel. Our **provisions** *were exhausted by this time, and for three days we had only salal berries and some soup made by thickening water, from flour shaken from a remaining flour sack, My uncle Levi Caffee, who was a great joker, looked at the poor mess and said to his wife, 'Why Ellen, ain't there a little bread or something.' 'Oh no,' she said, 'we are all starving together.'"*

You can read more of her memoir at this website.

Harriet Scott Palmer 🔍

pioneer: one of the first to settle in a new land.

disintegrate: to break down or decay.

irrigation: to provide water for crops through ditches, pipes, or other means.

transcontinental: across an entire continent.

WORDS TO KNOW

For many people, the Oregon Trail was more than just a trail to the West—it represented an opportunity for a new life, a better life.

However, the trail wasn't without risks. River crossings could be hazardous. The oxen pulling the settlers' wagons could drown or die from starvation or exhaustion. The **pioneers** also faced starvation, as well as disease. Another challenge? Shoes that **disintegrated** from too much use!

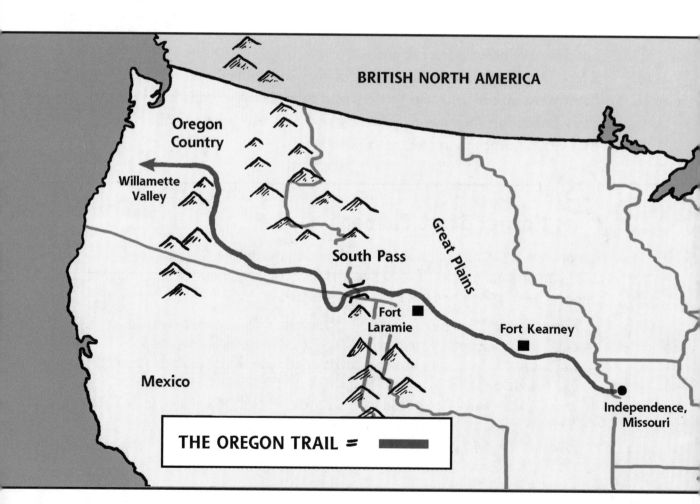

Western United States in 1840

For those wanting a piece of land, the 2,170-mile trail from Independence, Missouri, to the Willamette Valley in Oregon was worth the hardships. The 150-mile-long Willamette Valley is known for its good weather and mild winters. The soil is rich and rivers allow for **irrigation**. Farming was very productive in Willamette Valley, and this was a lifestyle many desired.

For the United States as a country, the Oregon Trail was invaluable. It allowed a young country to gain access to a wealth of natural resources and expand in a way that wouldn't have been possible otherwise. Eventually, the United States would double in size and become the third-largest nation in the world.

In *The Oregon Trail*, you'll learn about the first explorers to venture into the western wilderness, and read many stories of the people who followed in search of better lives. You'll learn about their hardships and successes and discover how the trail was only the first step on their journey to a new existence. You'll also learn the history of the **Transcontinental** Railroad, which finally removed the need for people to travel the Oregon Trail via foot, horseback, or wagon.

All aboard for an amazing journey along the Oregon Trail!

Good Study Practices

Every good historian keeps a history journal! As you read through this book and do the activities, keep track of your ideas and observations and record them in your history journal.

Each chapter of this book begins with an essential question to help guide your exploration of the Oregon Trail. Keep the question in your mind as you read the chapter. At the end of each chapter, use your history journal to record your thoughts and answers.

? ESSENTIAL QUESTION

Why did people risk traveling on the Oregon Trail if it was so dangerous?

PAINT THE OREGON TRAIL

In the 1800s, many artists used the American West as a canvas for artistic expression—George Catlin, Frederick Remington, and Charles Marion Russell are some of the most well known. Art of the American West presented the artist's perspective of specific events and or locations. Whether the subject was a cowboy, Native American, or a landscape, the paintings often conveyed deep emotion.

❯ **Visit the Simplot Art Collection of the Oregon Trail** at the National Oregon/California Trail Center in Montpelier, Idaho. This exhibit shows some of the work of artist Gary Stone, who created a panorama of the trail based on the diaries of immigrants. You can see some of these paintings at the website.

Oregon Trail Simplot Art 🔍

❯ **Search the Internet** or go to a favorite museum and look at more examples of Western art. What do you think of as you study the paintings? What emotions do you feel? How does the artist convey those emotions without using words?

❯ **Using art supplies you have on hand,** create your own work of art that illustrates what the American West and the Oregon Trail mean to you.

DID YOU KNOW?

Adolescent boys take between 12,000 and 16,000 steps a day and girls between 10,000 and 13,000 steps a day. The average number of steps in a mile are 2,000, so teens walk an average of five to eight miles a day. The Oregon Trail was approximately 2,170 miles. How long do you think it would take for you to walk it?

Chapter 1

A LAND **DEAL**

What do people do when there isn't enough room in their house for all the members of the family to eat, sleep, study, and play comfortably? Sometimes, they add on some space. Sometimes, they look for a new house!

While the people in the United States during the late 1700s and early 1800s felt that they needed more room, they weren't simply looking for a bigger house. They wanted a whole new, bigger piece of land and all of the resources that came along with it.

ESSENTIAL QUESTION

Why was the Louisiana Purchase important to the citizens of the United States?

In the early days of the United States, land was much more than the soil beneath your feet. Natural resources were **economic assets** that benefitted people. These resources included fertile land, water, plenty of fish, **mineral** deposits, timber, and wildlife. Land and its resources had value, both for individuals and for governments.

Ever since people began spreading out across the world, governments and private companies have invested in the exploration and claiming of land. History is filled with stories of battles and wars between countries as they struggled to take and keep the land they discovered. The United States was no different.

COLONIZATION: THE MIGHTY THREE

When Europeans began **colonizing** North America, three countries held most of the land. Great Britain claimed the East Coast and parts of Canada, France claimed the central area from Canada to the Gulf of Mexico, and Spain claimed what would become Florida, the American Southwest, and Mexico. Each of these three countries wanted more of the land, and wars broke out between them.

During the French and Indian War (1754–1763), Great Britain and France battled against each other for the right to own various pieces of land. When the war ended, France **ceded** much of its land in North America. Land east of the Mississippi River went to Great Britain. Land west of the Mississippi River went to Spain. But, as you'll see, it did not stay with Spain for long.

A LAND DEAL

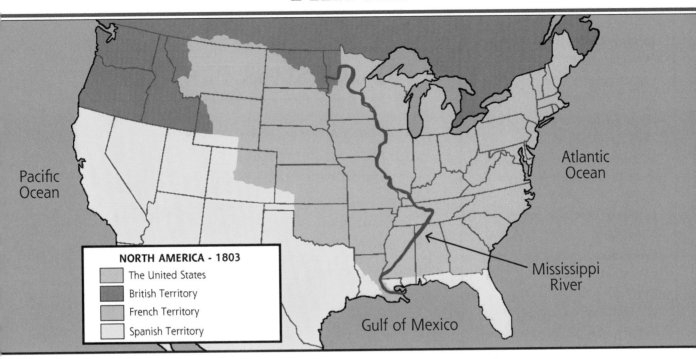

NORTH AMERICA - 1803
- The United States
- British Territory
- French Territory
- Spanish Territory

Pacific Ocean

Atlantic Ocean

Mississippi River

Gulf of Mexico

What do you know about the Revolutionary War (1775–1783)? You might know that this was a war fought because the **colonists** in America wanted independence from Great Britain. It was also a battle over land. When the war ended and the **Treaty** of Paris was signed in 1783, the United States added the Northwest **Territory** to the original colonies. The original Northwest Territory covered land north of the Ohio River between Pennsylvania's western border and the Mississippi River. This area later became Ohio, Indiana, Illinois, Michigan, and Wisconsin.

From 1846 to 1848, the United States and Mexico fought about the land from Texas to California in the Mexican-American War. The result of that war was that the United States gained the area that became the states of Texas, California, Nevada, Utah, Arizona, and New Mexico.

> **DID YOU KNOW?**
>
> The French and Indian War was known as the Seven Years' War in England and France.

What about today? Can you think of any wars being fought about land anywhere around the world?

land deal: a contract to buy or trade for land.

commerce: the activity of buying, selling, and trading.

rebellion: an act of open or violent resistance.

inflation: a rise in prices that leads to getting less for your money than you once got.

ratify: to officially approve something.

Congress: a group of people who represent the states and make laws for the country.

acquisition: something bought or gained.

WORDS TO KNOW

THE LOUISIANA PURCHASE

Not all land was won in battle. Some land was transferred in **land deals**. As the United States spread westward across the Appalachian Mountains, it claimed land in the Ohio River Valley and in areas including Kentucky and Tennessee. But President Thomas Jefferson had his eye on much more land, starting with the Mississippi River.

Owning this river would be a boost to the country's economy. It could be used to ship goods from the interior of the country to the port of New Orleans. The river and the port would greatly benefit American **commerce**.

Who owned this land? It was part of the Louisiana Territory. You can find it on the map on page 9. In 1762, after the French and Indian War, Spain and France signed a treaty that gave the Louisiana Territory to Spain. In 1795, the United States and Spain signed the Pinckney's Treaty, which allowed the United States to use the Mississippi River and the port of New Orleans. Spain also allowed Americans to live in New Orleans.

Meanwhile, the French Revolution raged in Europe. Napoleon, a successful military leader, wanted to restore France's presence on the North American continent. He wanted the Louisiana Territory back.

There was talk of a secret treaty in 1800 that would transfer ownership of the Louisiana Territory from Spain to France. When King Charles IV of Spain returned the Louisiana Territory to France in October 1802, the Spanish governor of New Orleans closed New Orleans to Americans.

Americans were furious! Some even called for war. Instead, President Jefferson, along with Secretary of State James Madison, began negotiations with France.

Jefferson sent Monroe to Paris in January 1803, when he learned that not all was going well with the French army. They were facing slave **rebellions** and disease in their Caribbean colonies and perhaps another war with Great Britain. The French could not afford to send its army to the Louisiana Territory, too. Might the United States be interested in buying Louisiana?

France agreed to sell the Louisiana Territory to the United States for $15 million, all 827,000 square miles of it, including the Mississippi River and New Orleans. Adjusting for **inflation**, that amount would be almost $306 million today. Still, it was a good deal—the United States paid only about 3¢ per acre.

The Louisiana Purchase treaty was **ratified** by **Congress** in October 1803 and the United States took possession of the territory on December 30, 1803.

Was it Legal?

The Louisiana Purchase was a controversial decision. The U.S. Constitution did not address the **acquisition** of territory. Some people questioned whether the Louisiana Purchase was legal. Many citizens, particularly those who lived in the territory, supported the purchase. President Jefferson, feeling that the benefits outweighed the drawbacks, proceeded with the sale for the good of the country. He asked the U.S. Senate to ratify the treaty with France. It did this on October 20, 1803, by a vote of 24 to 7.

THE BOUNDARIES OF THE LOUISIANA PURCHASE

When France sold the Louisiana Territory to the United States, no one was certain about its boundaries because it had never been **surveyed**. Everyone agreed on the eastern boundary, the Mississippi River, and that the southern boundary was the Gulf of Mexico, where New Orleans was located. But the Louisiana Purchase treaty didn't state boundaries as treaties often do. Instead it said, "the Colony or Province of Louisiana with the same extent it now has in the hands of Spain and that it had when France possessed it."

According to Thomas Jefferson, the Louisiana Purchase included all lands of the western **tributaries** of the Mississippi River, which included the then-unknown **headwaters** of the Missouri River. This would later be determined to be located in Montana.

DID YOU KNOW?

With the Louisiana Purchase, the United States doubled in size.

*"The geography of the Missouri and the most convenient water communication to the Pacific Ocean is a **desideratum** not yet satisfied."*
—Thomas Jefferson, July 3, 1803

For the next 20 years, the boundaries of the Louisiana Purchase were discussed, argued, and decided through treaty or **annexation**. Eventually, the territory stretched north to Canada and west to the Rocky Mountains. On the other side of the Rocky Mountains was the Pacific Northwest, claimed by Britain.

THE WAR OF 1812

The War of 1812 had the United States and Great Britain again arguing over boundaries. Although Great Britain officially recognized the United States, disagreements about trade and boundaries led to Congress declaring war on Great Britain on June 18, 1812.

U.S. forces fought well against the British, which were also fighting France on the European continent. After the British defeated Napoleon in 1814, they turned their full attention to the United States. Battles took place along the Canadian border, Atlantic Ocean, and Gulf Coast. Great Britain wanted to keep the United States from growing too big and powerful, while the United States wanted to expand its territory.

On August 24, 1814, the British marched into Washington, DC, and burned the Capitol, the White House, and other buildings to the ground. Things didn't look good, but the United States continued its defense.

prosperity: financial success.

latitude: the position of a place measured in degrees north or south of the equator.

Monroe Doctrine: the principle that any intervention by another country in the politics of the Americas is a potentially hostile act against the United States.

westward expansion: an event of mass migration to settle the American West.

manifest destiny: the belief that the United States had a mission to expand across North America.

WORDS TO KNOW

When the war ended in 1815, most of the boundaries were the same. Great Britain had increased its hold on Canada but the United States once again demonstrated that it was an independent country that deserved respect on the world's stage. Now, it was time to concentrate on growth and **prosperity**.

THE MONROE DOCTRINE & MANIFEST DESTINY

Who owned Oregon Country in the early nineteenth century? In addition to the Americans and British, both Spain and Russia had expressed interest in the land at times. In 1818, while serving as secretary of state, John Quincy Adams negotiated a treaty with Great Britain that established the U.S.-Canadian border at the 49th parallel, named after the circle of **latitude** there, but the boundary stopped at the Rocky Mountains.

Pirate or Patriot?

A popular resident of New Orleans was pirate Jean Lafitte. He was not as popular with governments, particularly the U.S. government. He was a pirate, after all. During the War of 1812, the British contacted Lafitte about aiding the British cause in the Gulf of Mexico. Lafitte decided he would benefit more by supporting the Americans. Andrew Jackson was in charge of defending the city. Jackson asked for Lafitte's assistance in the Battle of New Orleans. Lafitte offered arms and the assistance of his men, and the Americans won the Battle of New Orleans. Jean Lafitte and his men were given full pardons from the U.S. government.

The countries couldn't agree on boundaries west of the Rockies, but could agree to joint occupation of the land.

The following year, Spain ceded its claims to the Pacific Northwest. Russia, however, had granted its citizens fishing and whaling rights in the area. In 1823, President James Monroe made it known that the United States had a right to the land of the Pacific Northwest, based on earlier explorations. The United States would not tolerate colonization by Europe of this land.

This policy, known as the **Monroe Doctrine**, set the stage for **westward expansion**. Many Americans believed that their country's mission was to spread democracy and liberty to others. This **manifest destiny** included claiming land.

DID YOU KNOW?

During the War of 1812, Francis Scott Key wrote the national anthem, "The Star-Spangled Banner," after a battle at Fort McHenry in which the United States proved victorious.

What about the Native Americans, who had lived on the land long before any Europeans arrived? They were excluded from the promises and benefits of manifest destiny. Nineteenth-century policy was largely based on controlling Native Americans and removing them from the land they lived on, land that Americans wanted for themselves. Does this seem fair?

In 1846, the U.S. Senate gave Great Britain notice that the joint occupation agreement would expire in a year. Great Britain proposed extending the 49th parallel boundary west to the Pacific Ocean in exchange for Vancouver Island. While this is south of the 54th parallel that many had been pushing for, President James Polk agreed. He was facing problems with Mexico over the Southwest that would erupt in the Mexican-American War.

Oregon Country became Oregon Territory. It just needed American settlers. But first, explorers had to discover what this land might offer.

ESSENTIAL QUESTION

Now it's time to consider and discuss the Essential Question: Why was the Louisiana Purchase important to the citizens of the United States?

EXAMINE THE WORDS OF THOMAS JEFFERSON

"Under the law of nature, all men are born free, every one comes into the world with a right to his own person, which includes the liberty of moving and using it at his own will. This is what is called personal liberty . . . ."
—Thomas Jefferson

Thomas Jefferson was the third president of the United States, as well as a Founding Father and one of the primary authors of the Declaration of Independence. However, some people question the sincerity of a man who promoted liberty and freedom, yet owned slaves. In this activity, you will examine several quotes from Thomas Jefferson and explain what they mean.

❯ **Read some quotes attributed to Thomas Jefferson.** You can search by keyword or date, or simply browse the list.

❯ **Choose three quotes** that you believe still have meaning today. Look up any words you don't understand.

> Jefferson quotes family letters 🔍

❯ **Visually show each quote** along with what you believe Jefferson was trying to say. How would you rephrase the quote for today?

CONSIDER THIS: Some quotes attributed to Thomas Jefferson have never been verified. Look at these quotes. Why do you think these quotes came to be falsely connected to Thomas Jefferson?

> spurious quotations 🔍

DID YOU KNOW?

Newspaperman John L. O'Sullivan is credited with the term *manifest destiny*. He wrote that the United States "may confidently assume that our country is destined to be the great nation of futurity."

WRITE A TREATY

The United States has entered into hundreds of treaties. Treaties are also nothing new for the rest of the world. The United Nations calls treaties "the primary source of international law." The treaty section of the United Nations Office of Legal Affairs provides a treaty handbook to help people prepare treaties. What would you include in your own treaty? Remember, a treaty is a contract or agreement between two parties. It includes rules for both sides.

❯ **Look at examples of treaties** to see how they're written. You may want to refer to these sites.

❯ **After becoming familiar** with how treaties are written, write your own treaty. Brainstorm about situations in your life that a treaty could be used for. Ask yourself these questions.

Yale Law School Avalon Project 🔍

Search "treaties" at archives.gov 🔍

* What process would you go through in writing a treaty?

* Who is the treaty with?

* What needs to be in the treaty?

* What will you do if you and the other party don't agree on certain parts of the treaty?

* How will both parties agree to the treaty?

CONSIDER THIS: Treaties may be beneficial or have disadvantages depending on viewpoints and the effects of the treaties. Research examples of treaties that were not beneficial to certain populations.

What Is a Treaty?

A treaty is a formal, written agreement, usually created between two governments. Treaties often require much negotiation between parties. After the treaty is written, it must be approved and accepted by both sides. The United States requires that the Senate ratify any treaties that the United States enters into. During colonization, there were many treaties between countries. The United States also entered into many treaties with American Indian tribes or nations. Treaties often include some type of transfer, such as transfer of property or rights.

HOW DID THE LOUISIANA PURCHASE CHANGE AMERICA?

When France reacquired the Louisiana Territory in 1802, the United States became worried. American citizens had lived and worked in New Orleans for some time. The Mississippi River was also important to the economic growth of the country. President Thomas Jefferson said, "There is on the globe one single spot, the possessor of which is our natural and habitual enemy. It is New Orleans."

While people debated war, Jefferson and others were working behind the scenes to secure the Louisiana Territory for the United States. On July 4, 1803, President Jefferson announced the purchase of the Louisiana Territory from France. The territory would eventually become part or all of 15 states.

❱ **Read the Louisiana Purchase Treaty.**
You can find the full text of the document here.

Louisiana Purchase Treaty 🔍

❱ **Research and answer the following questions.**

✻ How did the Louisiana Purchase affect the United States?

✻ How do you think the Louisiana Purchase Treaty affected various groups of people, such as the **Federalists** and the people living in New Orleans?

✻ What affect did the Louisiana Purchase have on American trade?

❱ **Create a way to present your research.** Will you create a chart, a diagram, or a PowerPoint presentation? Consider the needs of your audience. What is the best way to show your information?

CONSIDER THIS: Although the Louisiana Purchase changed America, some people believed that Jefferson overstepped the authority he had as president. Many Federalists were against the purchase as well, believing it would anger the British, whom they wanted as **allies**. The U.S. House of Representatives voted to approve the Louisiana Purchase by just two votes. Do you think the Louisiana Purchase was a good idea or not? Explain your answer.

WORDS TO KNOW

Federalist: member of a political party during the late 1700s and early 1800s that favored a strong central government.

ally: a country that agrees to help and support another country.

MAPPING THE CHANGES
OF THE UNITED STATES

The United States started as a collection of colonies and territories. As time progressed, colonies and territories became states. The continental United States was completed with the admission of Arizona as the 48th state in 1912. By 1959, the last two states—Alaska and Hawaii—were admitted to the United States. In this activity, you will create maps of the United States at different points in time.

❯ **Research different types of historical U.S. maps.** The University of Texas has a digital collection here.

❯ **Choose five different representations** of the United States, such as:

> University of Texas US maps 🔍

* 1600s colonies
* Treaty of Paris, 1783
* Louisiana Purchase
* After the Civil War
* Modern times

❯ **Recreate the maps** digitally or through drawings. What does the progression of maps tell you about American history and settlement?

CONSIDER THIS: The United States shares boundaries with Canada and Mexico. What might politics be like if different boundaries had been established?

Latitude and Longitude

Everyone has an address. Most of us have a few addresses—email, home, and global. What's a global address? Everyone and everything on the earth has a global address. This is your latitude and **longitude**, the lines that circle the earth like a grid. Latitude lines run parallel to the equator. They measure the distance a place is from the equator. Longitude lines, known as meridians, run between the North and South Poles. They show how far east or west a location is from an imaginary line called the Prime Meridian, which runs through Greenwich, England.

WORDS TO KNOW

longitude: the position of a place measured in degrees east or west from the Prime Meridian line.

WHERE IN THE WORLD ARE YOU?

38.8895 degrees N, 77.0353 degrees W

If you put these coordinates into Google Maps or your phone, you would quickly find out that it is the location of the Washington Monument on the National Mall in Washington, DC. What do the numbers mean? The first number is always latitude. Latitude coordinates are between -90 degrees and 90 degrees or use N (North) or S (South). The equator is 0 degrees, so anything south of the equator will be a negative number or use S in the format.

The second number is always the longitude. It measures east or west from the Prime Meridian in Greenwich, England. Those numbers range from -180 degrees to 180 degrees, or they are written with a W for west of the Prime Meridian or E for east of the Prime Meridian.

❱ **Locate a globe or a map** with latitude and longitude lines. Examine the intersecting of lines. Why are coordinates useful?

❱ **Locate the 54-degree latitude.** People wanted this as the northern boundary of the Oregon Territory. Find the 49-degree latitude. How would the United States map look if the boundary had been set at 54 degrees?

❱ **Look at the following coordinates.** See if you can figure out the locations before entering the coordinates into a digital device to see where they are.

✱ 30 degrees N, 90 degrees W

✱ 45.5946 degrees N, 121.1787 degrees W

✱ 38.6247 degrees N, 90.1848 degrees W

✱ 55.9833 degrees S, 67.2667 degrees W

✱ 28.3852 degrees N, 81.5639 degrees W

✱ 48.8584 degrees N, 2.2945 degrees E

✱ 18.2871 degrees S, 147.699 degrees E

CONSIDER THIS: What are the coordinates for your home? School? Your favorite place to visit?

EXPLORING THE MONROE DOCTRINE AND MANIFEST DESTINY

"The American continents . . . are henceforth not to be considered as subjects for future colonization by any European powers."

On December 2, 1823, President James Monroe delivered his annual address to Congress about the changing relationship of the United States on the world stage. This included a warning that independent lands in the Western Hemisphere would be controlled by the United States. In addition, the United States would refrain from interfering in Europe.

In this activity, we will examine the words and intent of the Monroe Doctrine.

❯ **Read the transcript** of the Monroe Doctrine. Locate the few paragraphs that became known as the "Monroe Doctrine."

Monroe Doctrine 🔍

✱ Why do you think President Monroe decided to talk about colonization and independent lands in an address to Congress? Do you believe his history as a Founding Father was a factor?

✱ What do you think the reaction was from Congress? The American public? The British?

❯ **In current political times,** an opposing political party delivers a response to the first congressional address from a president. Write a response to this address from President Madison.

❯ **Manifest destiny** has been called a belief that the United States was entitled to expand. What is the relationship of the Monroe Doctrine to manifest destiny? Try visually representing the words—Monroe Doctrine—with the belief—manifest destiny.

CONSIDER THIS: The Monroe Doctrine has been called the cornerstone of American foreign policy. Do you believe American government has consistently followed the Monroe Doctrine? Provide examples. Can you think of any current events that follow the Monroe Doctrine?

WORDS TO KNOW

Western Hemisphere: the half of the earth that contains North and South America.

Chapter 2

EXPLORING
THE WEST

Curiosity is a strong human trait. We want to know what lies beyond the next boundary, whether that boundary is a mountain, river, or the atmosphere. What are you curious about? Where would you like to explore?

If you had lived during colonial times, you might have been curious about what lay west of the Appalachian Mountains. This was the first boundary of the colonies. British officials once prohibited settlement west of these mountains, but many settlers ignored this rule.

? ESSENTIAL QUESTION

What effect did the Lewis and Clark Expedition have on westward expansion?

frontier: the edge of what is settled.

game: wild animals hunted for sport or for food.

pelt: the skin or fur of an animal.

profit: the amount of money made after deducting expenses.

WORDS TO KNOW

By the early 1800s, the boundary of the United States had moved west, to the Mississippi River. People wondered what was on the other side of that boundary. They wanted to see it. Even more, they wanted to conquer it. Some of the first people to venture past the Mississippi River were fur trappers and traders.

FUR TRAPPERS AND TRADERS

Fur trade in the Pacific Northwest area began around 1780, when Captain James Cook of the British Navy became involved in trading sea otter fur. By the beginning of the nineteenth century, there were many land-based fur trappers. Many were French-Canadians, born and raised on the **frontier**. They were also called mountain men, because they lived off the land and knew their way around the wilderness. While fur trappers were explorers, their main reason for heading into the wilderness was to get rich.

In the early 1800s, the average beaver skin sold for $5 in St. Louis, Missouri. Today, that's approximately $144. Beaver were numerous and easy to trap. They only weighed about 1½ pounds, so a trapper could easily get several. And beavers were just one of many animals to trap or hunt. There were also lynx, fox, bears, deer, raccoons, elks, wolves, and bison.

Boone's Trace

A trader named John Finley told a young Daniel Boone of trading with Native American tribes west of the mountains. He described the plentiful **game** there. Daniel Boone blazed a route through the Cumberland Gap from Virginia to Kentucky, which made western travel possible. Originally known as a Native American trail called Warrior's Path, it became better known as Boone's Trace. Daniel Boone became one of the most popular folk heroes in American history.

Daniel Boone's cabin in High Bridge, Kentucky (Library of Congress)

Some early trappers worked independently and sold the **pelts** or traded them for goods in St. Louis. Some chose to try to get better prices by taking their business down the Mississippi River to New Orleans. Other fur trappers worked for trading companies. A company might provide a trapper with a horse, five traps, powder and lead for guns, knives, hatchets, and a kettle. The price of supplies was taken out of **profits**.

botany: the study of plants.

zoology: the study of animals.

staples: food or other products used regularly.

rations: someone's share of food.

WORDS TO KNOW

Fur trappers discovered different routes through the wilderness. Many were trails made by Native Americans. Often, fur trappers became friendly with area tribes, living among them and learning their languages. Experienced fur trappers became invaluable to exploring expeditions because they knew the land, the people, and, often, the language.

THE CORPS OF DISCOVERY

President Thomas Jefferson had long been interested in exploring the land west of the Mississippi, beyond the paths of trappers and traders. Spain had long refused permission for the Americans to explore the Louisiana Territory. Jefferson began making secret plans for an expedition. Even before the Louisiana Purchase became a reality, Thomas Jefferson was ready.

On January 18, 1803, Jefferson presented a proposal to Congress to fund an expedition to explore the territory that would double the size of the United States, as well as the area all the way to the Pacific Ocean. The cost? $2,500. The Corps of Discovery would form the core of the Lewis and Clark Expedition.

DID YOU KNOW?

We know about the many supplies purchased on the Lewis and Clark Expedition through copies of receipts. Learn more about supplies and equipment bought for this very important exploration at this site.

Lewis and Clark purchases 🔍

Jefferson told Congress that the expedition would build relationships with Native American tribes and promote commerce in the West. He also hinted at the importance of claiming territory before another country could do so. Funding for the Corps of Discovery was approved.

Unknown to Congress, Jefferson had already started preparations for exploration, appointing his personal secretary, Meriwether Lewis, as expedition leader. It was Lewis who had come up with the amount of $2,500 to put before Congress. But who would join him?

While in the military, Lewis had met William Clark, a man he greatly respected. Clark had moved to the Kentucky frontier at the age of 14 and picked up many useful skills by the time Lewis met him. Clark was the commanding officer of a unit of frontier riflemen. He was also an accomplished surveyor, mapmaker, and negotiator. A perfect addition to help lead the Corps of Discovery!

The Corps of Discovery would leave in the spring of 1804. While Meriwether Lewis increased his knowledge in the sciences, such as **botany** and **zoology**, he spent the year obtaining supplies. These included scientific and mathematical instruments, clothing, rifles, ammunition, camping and cooking equipment, and medicine.

Although the expedition would hunt and gather for food along the way, Lewis also bought **staples**, such as flour, sugar, salt, coffee, tobacco, and 100 gallons of whiskey. It was standard practice to include liquor in daily military **rations**.

Gifts for Native Americans included colorful glass beads, fishing hooks, scissors, blankets, and silver jewelry. Silver peace medals were also made. The medals, about 2 to 4 inches in diameter, had Jefferson's portrait engraved on one side. On the other were clasping hands and the words, "Peace & Friendship."

William Clark was assigned the task of choosing men. They wanted men with useful skills—hunting, tracking, **blacksmithing**, boating, and carpentry. Clark signed up two sergeants and seven privates before the group left for their winter camp north of St. Louis. Along the way, Clark picked up more men.

The men Clark hired were kept busy with camp chores, military drills, and shooting practice. Discipline was tight and some men had to be let go. One man who had no choice about the expedition was William Clark's black slave, York.

York's Journey

York (1770–1831) was born around the same time as William Clark, in 1770. They grew up together, and Clark often referred to York as his companion and servant. In truth, York began life as the property of William Clark's father, John Clark. When the father died, William Clark "inherited" York.

York was an important asset on the journey. Journal accounts describe him as an important team member who hunted, prepared food, and helped care for injuries. When Clark was lost in a flash flood, York went out in the storm to find him.

After the two-and-a-half-year expedition, York asked for his freedom, but Clark refused. York then asked to be returned to Kentucky so that he could be closer to his wife, who had a different owner. In 1809, Clark sent York to Kentucky, and sometime after 1815, he finally granted York his freedom.

York went into business hauling goods. He died of **cholera** sometime before 1832.

President Jefferson provided Meriwether Lewis with extensive instructions for the trip. Maps and detailed descriptions of people were of the highest importance. Jefferson also wanted information about **climate**, minerals, animals, soil, plants, and types of water. The Corps of Discovery set sail on the Missouri River on May 14, 1804.

DID YOU KNOW?

Aside from Lewis and Clark, George Drouillard (1774–1810) was the highest paid member of the team. The French-Canadian-Shawnee **interpreter** earned $25 a month.

THE LEWIS AND CLARK EXPEDITION

When Lewis and Clark set off on their journey, they were looking for a good route to the Pacific Coast. They focused on water routes. During the first six months, they traveled up the Missouri River, traveling 10 to 20 miles a day against river currents.

WORDS TO KNOW

specimen: a sample of something, such as plant material.

keelboat: a shallow freight boat.

pirogue: a long, narrow canoe.

landmark: an object in a landscape that can be seen from far away.

rapids: a part of a river where the current moves very fast.

Every day, the explorers rose early and ate cold leftovers from dinner before leaving camp. Lewis walked alongside the river collecting **specimens** and noting when they came to a good location for a settlement. Drouillard and a few men rode out on horses to hunt game and gather wild plants. Clark usually stayed with the boats, a **keelboat** and two **pirogues**, which held their gear. He took compass readings and recorded **landmarks** for mapping purposes.

The remainder of the men were assigned the duty of getting the boats up river. It was a difficult job going against the current. They often faced **rapids** and dangers lurking just below the surface, such as sharp rocks and tree trunks. At times, the men had to use tow ropes to pull the boats up the Missouri River. Lewis and Clark spent evenings updating maps and journals while team member Pierre Cruzatte entertained the men with his fiddle.

DID YOU KNOW?

Meriwether Lewis felt that an exploring team needed a dog. A large, black Newfoundland named Seaman joined the crew. His main activities were diving into the water to chase beaver, although he also caught an antelope once.

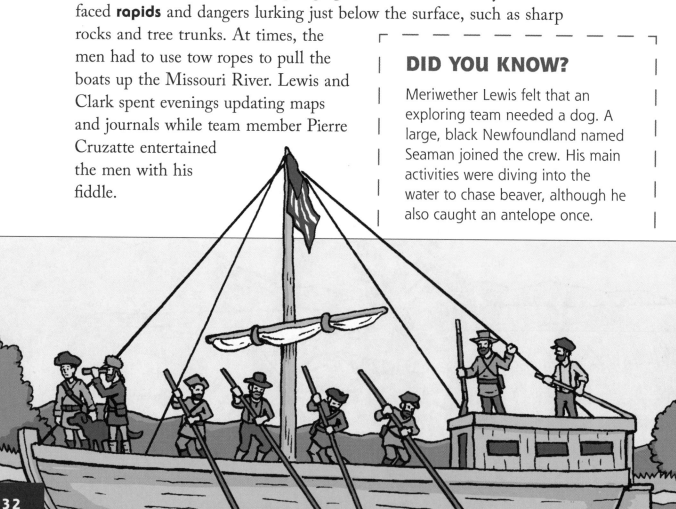

When they entered the Great Plains, it was a sea of grass where large herds of buffalo, elk, and deer lived. There were animals they had never seen before, such as long-eared jackrabbits and yipping coyotes.

Lewis was fascinated with prairie dogs. He called them "barking squirrels." The men captured one to send to President Jefferson.

The expedition sought out Native American tribes along the way. Through interpreters and sign language, they explained that the French and Spanish "fathers" were gone, but that an American chief—Thomas Jefferson—now led them all. The team showed the native people special tools, such as guns, compasses, and magnifying glasses. And they offered the people gifts. Most of the time, the meetings went fairly well, although were some tense moments, such as occurred with the Lakota and Blackfeet tribes.

The Lewis and Clark Expedition stopped to make its winter camp near present-day Bismarck, North Dakota, across from a Mandan village. They sent a small group of men back down the river with the keelboat filled with specimens and copies of maps and journals for President Jefferson. The remainder of the men camped for the next five months until the spring thaw came. Although they had traveled 1,600 miles, there were still many miles to go.

Expedition Journals

So much is known about the journey of the Lewis and Clark Expedition due to the journals kept by the men. Lewis and Clark weren't the only men to record their adventures. Journals were also kept by Sergeants Charles Floyd, Patrick Gass, and John Ordway, and Private Joseph Whitehouse. You can search the journal entries by writers and dates at this website.

PBS journal search 🔍

Continental Divide: the imaginary line that separates river systems flow to opposite sides of a continent.

WORDS TO KNOW

SACAGAWEA JOINS THE TEAM

While planning for the next part of their journey, Lewis and Clark hired another interpreter. French fur trader Toussaint Charbonneau (1760–1843) was from Montreal, Canada. His wife, Sacagawea (1788–1812), was Shoshone. She had been taken from her people by Charbonneau when she was 12 years old. Lewis and Clark knew they would be meeting Shoshone in their travels, and Sacagawea would be able to interpret for them.

Sacagawea proved to be great help to the expedition. She had a good knowledge of plants and the land. According to Clark's journal, Sacagawea responded calmly in all situations, even in the case of overturned boats, unlike her husband and some of the other men. In addition to interpreting, her presence reassured other Native Americans that the expedition meant no harm.

One more member of their family also made the journey—their newborn son, Jean Baptiste Charbonneau. Clark was very fond of the child and called him Pomp, or Pompey.

DID YOU KNOW?

Ticks and mosquitoes were a problem on the expedition. The men spread grease on their bodies as protection against the pests.

MORE MILES TO EXPLORE

On April 7, 1805, 33 people set off in six small canoes and two large pirogues. They faced grizzly bears, strong rapids, and the unknown. Within six weeks, they got their first glimpse of the Rocky Mountains. But for Lewis, that didn't compare to the rapid, rocky series of waterfalls that Great Falls, Montana, would get its name from. It was "the grandest sight I ever beheld."

The expedition had to pull out of the water and travel by land. They built wagon frames from cottonwood trees and set the boats on them. Without horses, the men had to pull the wagons.

Captains Lewis & Clark holding a Council with the Indians   *Page 17*

The journals of Lewis and Clark describe meeting with various Native American tribes on their journey west. (Library of Congress)

By July 25, after crossing the two-mile Lemhi Pass between present-day Montana and Idaho, they reached another milestone—the **Continental Divide**. This imaginary line marks a kind of boundary in the continent. Rivers east of the Continental Divide flow east, while rivers west of the divide flow west.

Water travel should have become easier since they would now be following the current, but the rivers were still too rough to travel safely. The expedition met the Shoshone, and with Sacagawea's help, Lewis and Clark were able to trade for 30 horses.

WORDS TO KNOW

elevation: a measurement of height above sea level.

frostbite: an injury from prolonged exposure to extreme cold.

WORDS TO KNOW

Even with horses, traveling along the 200-mile Lolo Trail proved difficult. The high **elevations** and narrow trails were blanketed with cold rain, hail, and snow. Food and water were scarce and expedition members suffered from **frostbite**.

Clark wrote, "I have been wet and as cold in every part as I ever was in my life."

When they reached a Nez Perce village on the other side, they made five dugout canoes. Travel was easier at times as they moved with the current of the Clearwater and Snake Rivers.

The Snake River is a tributary of the fourth largest river by volume in the United States, the Columbia River, which empties into the Pacific Ocean. As members of the Lewis and Clark Expedition followed the Columbia River, they saw another landmark, Mount Hood, the highest mountain in Oregon.

The travelers navigated another series of rapids and waterfalls now known as The Dalles. The Columbia River eventually widened into a bay that emptied into the Pacific Ocean.

They had made it across the wilderness to the far ocean. It was late November. They could do more exploring, start the return journey, or camp for the winter. Lewis and Clark let the team vote. Every member of the party was allowed to vote.

Neither York nor Sacagawea would live long enough to see African Americans or Native Americans obtain the right to vote, but in the Lewis and Clark camp, their voices were heard along with everyone else's.

DID YOU KNOW?

The expedition encountered a variety of environments along their route—desert, prairies, and even rainforests.

The group voted to build a winter camp on the south side of the Columbia River. They named it Fort Clatsop after a nearby tribe.

The Astorians

John Jacob Astor (1763–1848) was the head of the American Fur Company and the richest man in America of his time. He sent two groups to the Pacific Northwest, one by water and one by land. These travelers were known as Astorians.

The *Tonquin* set sail from New York in September 1810. It sailed south, all the way around the southern tip of South America, before turning north to sail along the west coasts of South America and North America. The group reached its destination of the mouth of the Columbia River a little more than six months later and began building a fur-trading post, Fort Astor.

The overland expedition wasn't as lucky. The members lost their supplies and had to walk much of the way. The men even ate their own moccasins to avoid starvation. They arrived in Astoria almost a year after they had started, and didn't find many people waiting for them. The *Tonquin* had been attacked by the Salish at Vancouver Island. Reportedly, the last remaining crewman blew up the ship with the warriors on board.

THE JOURNEY HOME

The group spent the winter repairing and cleaning equipment. In March 1806, after giving Fort Clatsop to the Clatsop tribe, the expedition started its return journey. The party had to rest with the Nez Perce in late spring until more snow melted in the mountains.

After crossing the mountains, the members decided to split up, with Lewis heading one group and Clark the other. If both were successful, they'd meet at the Missouri River. Lewis took an overland route told to him by a Shoshone guide. This allowed him to explore farther north.

The difficult part of the route had taken about five months the year before. But with new knowledge, both Lewis and Clark took less that six weeks.

Clark's group traveled the Yellowstone River through the Rockies with the help of Sacagawea. He wrote, "At 4PM [I] arrived at the remarkable rock situated in an extensive bottom. This rock I ascended and from its top had a most extensive view in every direction." He named the group of sandstone formations Pompey's Tower after Sacagawea's son and carved his name and date into the sandstone. Today, it is known as Pompey's Pillar.

On August 12, 1806, Lewis and Clark were reunited. Two days later, Sacagawea, Charbonneau, and their son returned to their home.

William Clark's name carved into Pompey's Tower
(Bureau of Land Management)

After saying goodbye to Sacagawea and her family, the Lewis and Clark Expedition traveled down the Missouri River. This time, they sailed with the current and the trip went quickly—they traveled up to 70 miles a day.

They arrived in St. Charles, Missouri, on September 23, 1806, after traveling 7,680 miles. They'd been gone for two and a half years and, in that time, many people assumed the expedition members had died. Instead, Lewis and Clark became national heroes.

When they returned home, expedition members received double pay and 320 acres of land. Lewis and Clark each received 1,600 acres. Lewis became governor of the Louisiana Territory, but died three years later of a gunshot wound under mysterious circumstances. Clark lived for 32 more years, serving for a time as governor of the Missouri Territory.

The Corps of Discovery added to the knowledge of the West. It also proved that crossing the continent could be done.

The intrepid explorers and traders of the early nineteenth century set the stage for the westward expansion of the United States. Because of them, a mass **migration** of people was possible. They were able to go west in search of new land, new lives, and wealth.

ESSENTIAL QUESTION

Now it's time to consider and discuss the Essential Question: What effect did the Lewis and Clark Expedition have on westward expansion?

PRESERVING PLANTS

President Jefferson described botany as "among the most useful of the sciences." He was said to own more than 30 books on botany and was something of an expert on the botany of Virginia. Learning about the plants was a key task for Lewis and Clark. In preparation, Lewis studied botany and learned how to collect specimens. He sent 198 dried specimens during their first winter at Fort Mandan and brought back more at the end of the journey. Some of the specimens Meriwether Lewis preserved were Osage orange tree and food crops grown by Native Americans, including Indian corn varieties, plains coneflower, and snowberry bush.

NOTE: In this activity, you will learn how to preserve plants. Make certain you have permission to pick plants before doing so.

❯ **Look for some type of plant guide** or app that will allow you to identify plants before picking them. You don't want to accidentally collect poison ivy!

❯ **Pack your collecting gear.** What do you think you'll need? You might want to include:

* Scissors

* Newspaper

* Spray bottle of water

❯ **Choose specimens.** Place individual specimens between sheets of damp newspaper.

❯ **When you return home,** choose a location for drying the plants. The process takes about three weeks.

* Lay several sheets of dry newspaper both under and above plant specimens.

* Place a flat board on top of the newspapers. Weigh it with something heavy, such as books.

* For the first 10 days, replace the newspapers on top of the specimens with dry newspapers every day. Carefully move plants with tweezers every few days.

* After 10 days, leave the plants between the newspapers without disturbing them until they are completely dry.

CONSIDER THIS: Decide how you want to display the plants. Do you want to use clear, sealable bags? Mount your specimens on poster board? What are some other ideas? How will you label them?

What's in a Plant's Name?

According to the Botanic Gardens Conservation International, the first list of plant **species** in the world was completed in 2010. Of the 1 million plant species names on the list, only about 350,000 are accepted names. Another 470,000 names are synonyms of accepted Latin names. That leaves more than 242,000 plant species names currently "unresolved." Why do you think it might be difficult for there to be agreement on plant names?

WORDS TO KNOW

species: a group of living things that are closely related and can produce offspring.

MAPPING LEWIS AND CLARK
AND THE OVERLAND ASTORIANS

Lewis and Clark traveled more than 7,000 miles. Sections of their journey and that of the Astorians in 1811 became part of the Oregon Trail. In this activity, you will recreate the routes of these early explorers.

❱ **Take a look at the interactive map here.** You can trace Lewis and Clark traveling west in red and the return trip in blue.

PBS Corps Discovery map 🔍

❱ **Find maps of the route** the Astorian group took west, such as the one here.

NPS Astorian map 🔍

❱ **Compare and contrast the routes.** Keep track of your observations in a chart, like the one below.

✱ What parts of the routes are the same?

✱ What types of **geographic** features possibly helped or hindered their journeys?

❱ **Present your research.** Will you create a chart, a diagram, or a PowerPoint presentation? Consider the needs of your audience. What is the best way to show your information?

Route	Geographic Features	Dangers	Ease of Travel	Distance

CONSIDER THIS: If you were an explorer, what route would you have taken and why? Would you follow Lewis and Clark, the Astorians, or come up with a new route?

WORDS TO KNOW

geographic: the physical features of an area.

CREATE A STORYBOARD
OF SACAGAWEA'S LIFE

Lewis and Clark might not have been as successful as they were without Sacagawea. Clark's journals are full of praise for the young Shoshone woman whom he sometimes referred to as their "pilot." However, except for her time with the expedition, little is known about her brief life. In this activity, you will examine information about Sacagawea and create a storyboard on one aspect of her life.

❯ **Investigate resources** about the life of Sacagawea. Possible sources include expedition journals and sites such as these.

❯ **Review each source** with the following considerations.

PBS Corps of Discovery, Sacagawea 🔎

Lewis and Clark National Historic Trails 🔎

✱ Is the information presented as fact or guesses?

Nebraska 🔎

✱ Did you learn anything you didn't know before?

Lemhi-Shoshone Tribe 🔎

✱ How does the source of the material affect what you read?

❯ **Choose an event** in the life of Sacagawea to visually represent in a storyboard. Storyboards are often used to plan videos. They are a series of drawings that visually represent scenes and sometimes dialogue in order.

CONSIDER THIS: If you were going to shoot Sacagawea's life as a video, what would you choose as the opening scene?

DID YOU KNOW?

Wagon wheel ruts of the Oregon Trail can still be seen in some places, more than 160 years after it was traveled. The trail lay through six states.

Missouri: 16 miles

Wyoming: 491 miles

Kansas: 165 miles

Idaho: 510 miles

Nebraska: 424 miles

Oregon: 524 miles

Chapter 3

NEW BEGINNINGS

The Lewis and Clark Expedition created much excitement about the West. Many people wanted to see it for themselves. Many were willing to take their chances getting there for a better life. The land between the Rocky Mountains and the Pacific Ocean was referred to as Oregon Country. It included present-day Oregon, Washington, and parts of Idaho and British Columbia.

It was still a difficult journey filled with too many challenges for the average pioneer family. In the years following the Lewis and Clark Expedition, traffic was limited to mainly fur trappers, traders, and adventurers. Concerns over Indian attacks prompted exploration of other routes.

? ESSENTIAL QUESTION

What had to happen before people could begin traveling the Oregon Trail?

recede: to become more distant or move away.

WORDS TO KNOW

Perhaps the biggest challenge was crossing the Rocky Mountains and the Continental Divide. Lewis and Clark had traveled over rocky ridges at high elevations in extreme weather conditions. How could families traveling by wagon make it over these narrow trails? There had to be a better way.

THE SOUTH PASS

Robert Stuart (1785–1848) was a partner in the American Fur Company, and had helped establish Astoria on the Pacific Coast. In 1812, he was chosen to lead a small group of men back East to report on the problems the Pacific Fur Company was facing against the British fur-trading companies.

Stuart planned to retrace a route that followed the Columbia and Snake Rivers. But because of a threat of Indian attack near Union Pass, the group traveled farther south to look for a pass that Stuart had heard about from a Native American guide. They located a wide pass covered in grass and sagebrush. On September 12, 1812, he wrote in his journal:

> *"Immediately on leaving our last night's station, the country opened very much to the South, the mountains **receded** to a great distance and a beautiful low Plain occupied the intervening space."*

The pass, ranging from 12 to 20 miles wide, was located between the Wind River Range and the Antelope Hills. At only 7,440 feet above sea level, the increase in elevation was barely noticeable. Paths to the north were at least twice as high and rocky. It became known as South Pass, because it was south of Lolo Pass, where Lewis and Clark had crossed over the Continental Divide. Trips that crossed the continent via South Pass could cut travel time to Oregon Country in half. Look on the map on page vi to see the South Pass.

overlander: a person who traveled over land to the western United States.

missionary: a person sent by a church to persuade others to join or practice a specific religion.

mission: a church where missionaries live and work.

advocate: a person who speaks out in support of someone or something.

WORDS TO KNOW

Robert Stuart's journal included a complete description of their route. But John Jacob Astor, owner of the American Fur Company and Stuart's employer, considered Stuart's journal private business information. He kept the information about South Pass to himself until years later, when he turned over the journal to Washington Irving for the writing of the book, *Astoria*.

South Pass was rediscovered 12 years later by 25-year-old Jedediah Smith (1798–1831). Originally from Virginia, Smith arrived in the area to trap beaver on the Upper Missouri River. When asked to lead a group of trappers to Oregon Country, he accepted and led them over South Pass, which he learned about from the Crow people.

Historians say that the settlement of the West might never have happened without South Pass. It was the key to the Oregon Trail.

DID YOU KNOW?

Stuart's journal wouldn't be published until he had been dead for almost 100 years.

EARLY PIONEERS ON THE OREGON TRAIL

The word *pioneer* probably originated from old French words *peonier* or *pionier*, meaning "foot soldier." When the many steps from Missouri to Oregon Territory are added up, the pioneers of the Oregon Trail were indeed foot soldiers.

But most people who traveled the 2,200-mile Oregon Trail were referred to as **overlanders**. This was because they were traveling over land instead of by ship.

Missionaries were some of the earliest people on the Oregon Trail. After a meeting with four Native American men, William Clark reported that they had asked for someone to teach their people about the white man's powerful book. Clark took this to mean the Bible and forwarded the request to the Methodist Missionary Board. This led to some people making the journey in order to teach others about the Methodist religion.

Methodist-Episcopalian missionary Jason Lee (1803–1845) of Canada made a successful journey on the Oregon Trail with fur trader Nathaniel Wyeth in 1834. Lee established the first **mission** near the Willamette River. He was an **advocate** of increasing settlement, and to accomplish this, he made trips Back East to encourage others.

(PS) Go West, Young Man

A popular nineteenth-century phrase was "Go West, Young Man, Go West." John Babsone Lane Soule of *The Terre Haute Express* first used it in 1851. Horace Greeley, editor of the *New York Tribune*, popularized it when he used it in an editorial on July 13, 1865. He wrote, "Go West, young man, and grow up with the country."

Five men at a fort or trading post along the Oregon Trail in 1851–1852 (Library of Congress)

Two years after Lee's first journey, more missionaries set out with Hudson's Bay Company fur traders. This group included the first white women to travel the trail—Narcissa Whitman (1808–1847), along with her new husband, Dr. Marcus Whitman (1802–1847), and Eliza Spalding (1807–1851), with her husband, Reverend Henry Spalding (1803–1874).

Most people at the time doubted that women could make the journey.

At Fort Hall, the group had to follow pack trails on horseback the rest of the way. There weren't wagon trails yet. The Spaldings established their mission near the Nez Perce in the Lapwai Valley. The mission eventually included a school and printing house.

By 1843, the Oregon Trail would pass by Whitman Mission, just north of today's Oregon-Washington state line. The Whitmans sent letters back East to tell of the many benefits of the West. For the next 10 years, they greeted the many pioneers who passed by their front door on their way to their own land. They also helped the numerous people who stopped due to hunger, illness, or other difficulties.

Missionaries weren't the only people who migrated for religious reasons. The Mormons were people who wanted to establish their own religious-based government. They traveled part of the Oregon Trail on their way to the Great Salt Lake area in Utah, beginning in 1847. The missionaries and others who made these first trips proved that wagons could make the journey.

THE GREAT MIGRATION

Traveling with a group of fur traders, Joel Walker migrated with his wife, sister-in-law, and five children to Oregon Country in 1840. The next year, the Bidwell-Bartleson Party traveled with Jesuit missionaries. Although the original plan was to travel to California, the group split, with half going to Oregon and half to California. In both cases, the wagons had to be abandoned and the people completed the journey on foot.

Letters from the Oregon Trail

The Whitmans and the Spaldings crossed South Pass on July 3, 1836. On the following day, they stopped at Pacific Springs with a Bible in one hand and the American flag in another and claimed Oregon Country for the United States.

Eliza Spalding said the moment gave her strength.

"Is it reality or a dream that after four months of hard and painful journeying I am alive, and actually standing on the summit of the Rocky Mountains, where yet the foot of white woman has never trod."

Two years later, four more female missionaries traveled the Oregon Trail on horseback—Myra Fairbanks Eells, Mary August Dix Gray, Sarah Gilbert White Smith, and Mary Richardson Walker.

Narcissa Whitman sent detailed letters about both her journey and life at the Whitman Mission. You can read more of Whitman's letters here.

Narcissa Whitman letters 🔍

WORDS TO KNOW

Great Migration: the mass movement of people to the West in the nineteenth century.

emigrant: a person who leaves one country or region to settle in another. Before Oregon and California were officially part of the United States, pioneers were called emigrants.

undercarriage: the framework underneath a vehicle, such as a wagon

axle: the shaft on which a pair of wheels rotates.

Every time people heard of someone who had successfully made the trek over the Oregon Trail, it ignited the dreams of others looking for land and opportunities. Americans had caught "Oregon fever."

Nearly 1,000 people gathered at Independence, Missouri, in the spring of 1843 to travel on the Oregon Trail. It was the largest group yet to travel, with approximately 120 wagons and 5,000 cattle. This long wagon train was the beginning of the **Great Migration**.

Twice as many people traveled the Oregon Trail the following year. Within a few years, more than 5,000 people had made the trek.

EMIGRANTS AND IMMIGRANTS

Early overlanders weren't just pioneers. They were also **emigrants** leaving their country to settle in Oregon Country. When the Napoleonic Wars ended in Europe in the 1820s, large numbers of Europeans immigrated to the United States. Half of the population of Ireland immigrated due to hardships of starvation in the Great Famine.

Approximately 1 million Irish people died from the famine, caused by a disease that destroyed the potato crop.

Pioneers could be emigrants and immigrants. Places such as Ireland and Germany saw the people leaving as emigrants. But to the United States, they were immigrants, people who decided to settle in America.

Anatomy of a Prairie Schooner

Wagons were one of the main ways to move cargo until the use of trains. One type of wagon used in the eastern United States was a large covered wagon known as the Conestoga wagon. But in the trails heading west, travelers needed a smaller, lighter wagon that could travel uneven and narrow roads. This lighter wagon became known as the prairie schooner. With its white bonnet moving across the prairies, it resembled the sails of a ship or schooner.

The base of a prairie schooner was a wooden bed about 4 feet wide and 10 feet long. A box at one end, called a jockey box, held tools. The wooden bed sat on an **undercarriage** atop the wheels and **axles**. Hanging from the back axle was a bucket of tallow and tar to be used to grease wheels and axles to keep them moving well. Above the bed, a curved canvas stretched over wooden bows. The canvas tied onto the sides of the bed.

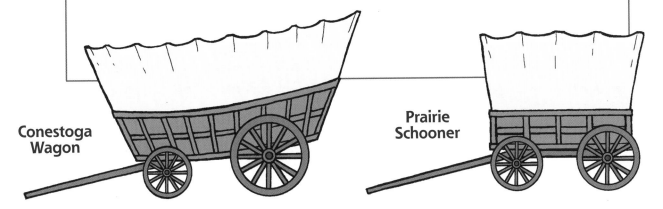

Conestoga Wagon

Prairie Schooner

More than 7 million immigrants arrived in the United State between 1820 and 1870. Irish and German immigrants made up two-thirds of that number. They arrived in cities on the East Coast. Finding a place to live and a job with decent wages could be challenging. Many, particularly those drawn by the idea of owning their own land, looked to the West.

AFRICAN AMERICANS

Although York, Lewis's slave, was the first African American to make the overland trip to the Oregon Territory, more followed in his footsteps. Some were also slaves who worked for fur traders or white pioneers.

But there were also free African Americans who journeyed on the Oregon Trail.

Many **territorial** governments banned slavery, but some settlers wanted to keep the Oregon Territory a "white" territory. The first **exclusion law**, adopted in 1844, ordered that all slaves be set free. But it also stated that African Americans attempting to settle in Oregon were to be publicly whipped—39 lashes—every six months until leaving. There is no record of the law being used and it was **repealed** in 1857.

One African American settler was named George W. Bush (1779–1863). The "W" was rumored to stand for "Washington." He had fought under Andrew Jackson in the Battle of New Orleans and was successful at trading cattle in Missouri. With a wife and five children, he was ready to give his family a new start in the Pacific Northwest.

The Donner Party

It may be possible that some of the overlanders on the Oregon Trail met or exchanged words with a family known as the Donners. The Donners traveled part of the Oregon Trail on their way to California. The Donner Party was a group of 81 men, women, and children who started on the Oregon Trail in 1846. Following advice from a guide, they took a "shortcut" that put them way behind schedule. They were almost out of food when they reached the Sierra Nevada mountains in California in late October. A devastating early blizzard trapped them high in the mountains for five months. Nearly half died. A rumor that some of the members of the party resorted to eating the dead persists even today.

In 1844, Bush and his family joined a wagon train bound for the Columbia River Valley. He was among the most prosperous, owning six of the wagons. Other overlanders in the group would have likely starved without Bush, who was a great help to the 84-wagon train. By the time they reached Fort Bridger in Wyoming, many of them were out of supplies. Bush bought flour, sugar, and calico so that people were fed and clothed. He also taught people how to hunt wild game. His advice was that anything larger than a blackbird could be killed and eaten.

The Oregon exclusion law said Bush couldn't settle in Oregon, so he and his family went to Puget Sound, which was still under British control. They were joined by four or five of the white families that had traveled with them, including Michael T. Simmons, an Irish immigrant. Bush operated a successful farm that supplied many newcomers with food. In 1845, he introduced the first sawmill and **gristmill** in the area.

DID YOU KNOW?

During the years of the Great Migration, more than 3 million African Americans were held in slavery in the South.

George Washington (1817–1905)

George W. Bush is sometimes confused with another African American pioneer. George Washington was the son of a white mother and an African American slave, but was raised by a white foster family. In 1850, he was frustrated with the limits on his freedom in Missouri. He joined a wagon train heading west. When he was refused the right to own land in the Oregon Territory, he moved north of the Columbia River to the Washington Territory.

George Washington was described as a **jack-of-all trades**. He participated in many businesses and was usually successful at them. In 1875, when there was news that the Northern Pacific Railroad would be building a railway, Washington established a town. First named Centerville, it was later renamed Centralia. He and his wife donated land for a church, cemetery, and city park.

When the country was hit by a financial depression in 1893, Washington bought food at **wholesale** prices to provide to residents of the town. He also held the **mortgages** for those who were bankrupt until they were able to repay the loans. Today, Centralia is home to more than 16,000 people.

After the United States and British governments agreed on the boundary at the 49th parallel, it placed Bush back under the discriminatory Oregon law. Because of this, Bush no longer held clear title to his land. Simmons, who was elected to the Oregon territorial legislature in 1854, sponsored a bill to **exempt** Bush from the exclusion law and to grant him a homestead. The measure passed, and Bush was legally granted 640 acres. Today, his homestead is known as Bush Prairie.

Another African American settler was Louis Sansworth (1830–1917), who was 23 years old when his owner brought him to Oregon. Sansworth entertained the travelers along the way with his violin. Settling near gold fields in southern Oregon, Sansworth began earning money through mining to purchase his freedom. When he realized he could earn more with his music, he traded in his mining pick and began playing at dances and teaching violin.

It took Sansworth six years to purchase his freedom. He remained in Oregon for the rest of his life.

When the Oregon Constitution was adopted in 1857, it banned slavery, but made it illegal for African Americans to own property, vote, or engage in legal contracts. This amendment did not apply to African Americans already living in Oregon. How did these laws keep African Americans from prospering in the same way as the white settlers?

The early pioneers helped established a path that thousands more would follow in search of better lives. Some would find those better lives, but the journey on the Oregon Trail was an incredibly difficult one that even the most **stalwart** overlander found challenging.

ESSENTIAL QUESTION

Now it's time to consider and discuss the Essential Question: What had to happen before people could begin traveling the Oregon Trail?

KEEP A JOURNAL

Have you ever kept a journal or diary? Many people who traveled the Oregon Trail kept written accounts of their experiences. And it's those accounts that help us understand what life was like in the nineteenth century. We know Robert Stuart was the first white person to discover the South Pass because he wrote about it in his journal. If he hadn't kept a journal and documented his travels, we would never know this. Let's explore some diaries.

❯ **Look at some journal entries** written on the Oregon Trail. You can do an Internet search to find examples at websites such as these.

✱ What's the difference between diaries and journals?

Oregon Trail Center journals 🔎

✱ Is it just a matter of word choice?

Oregon pioneer journals 🔎

✱ If so, what word would you choose and why?

❯ **Have you ever heard of** *The Diary of Anne Frank*? Most people have. Through it, we know about one girl's brief life during the Holocaust. Can you think of other famous diaries or journals? Today, many people write travel blogs to share their experiences about trips. Write a sample travel blog about a day on the Oregon Trail.

CONSIDER THIS: The next time you take a trip, consider keeping a journal of your travels. Write down details of your daily activities and things that you see. Why might a travel journal be useful?

Journals and Diaries: A Glimpse into the Past

What is the difference between a diary and a journal? Very little! Both are records of a fixed time. In nineteen-century America, they were both quite common, particularly for people making the long trip west. Journals were often a log of how many miles had been traveled, supplies used, and descriptions of landmarks that might prove helpful to future travelers. Diaries were often more personal accounts that described more than just the facts.

POLITICAL CARTOONING

Our beliefs about political issues are often influenced by what we see and hear. Political cartoons are one way of conveying political messages. This activity will explore the persuasive techniques of political cartoons.

❯ **Most people like comics,** but political cartoons aren't necessarily funny.

✱ Why do we have political cartoons?

✱ What is the purpose of a political cartoon?

✱ Who is a political cartoon's audience?

❯ **"War! Or No War"** is the title of this political cartoon held by the U.S. Library of Congress. Originally published in 1846, the cartoon has two Irish immigrants debating the boundary of the Oregon Territory. One character says, "Ike! say the 49th & let's settle it amercably." The other answers, "No Sir-ree I goes for the hull of Oregon or none—I do & don't do nor-thin else."

❯ **Analyze the message** of the "War! Or no war" cartoon. What does this single panel tell you?

❯ **Examine modern political cartoons.** Ask the following questions.

✱ What is the subject of the cartoon?

✱ What is the cartoon's message?

✱ How does the artist represent a situation, event, or belief without words?

CONSIDER THIS: Draw your own political cartoon. It can be about a global issue, a national issue, or perhaps a local issue. Maybe your subject will be something that is meaningful to people your age.

┌ ─ ─ ─ ─ ─ ─ ─ ─ ─ ─ ─ ┐

DID YOU KNOW?

The first political cartoon is believed to be "Join, or Die," published in *The Pennsylvania Gazette* in 1754. The artist? Founding Father Benjamin Franklin!

Join, or Die 🔍

WRITE A LETTER

Have you ever received a letter in the mail? It has become rarer in the twenty-first century to write and receive letters. People are more likely to communicate with people from all around the world through the Internet or on a cellphone. But before modern communication, people wrote letters to family and friends who lived far away. Letters were filled with news, and to receive one was very exciting.

When people began traveling west, letter writing was an important way to stay connected and to learn about new places. Many people worked on a letter for weeks or even months, adding things to it until it was ready to mail.

❯ Read some examples of pioneer letters. How do they describe life on the Oregon Trail?

❯ Imagine that you're a pioneer. You left your best friend behind, and you don't

American memory prairie letters 🔎

know when or if you'll ever see them again. Write a letter to your friend with three parts.

✱ Describe traveling on the Oregon Trail.

✱ Describe your first look at your new home.

✱ Describe what your new life is like after three months.

CONSIDER THIS: Much of what we know about the Oregon Trail and the people who traveled it are because of the letters they wrote and journals they kept. How would we know about this part of history if we didn't have access to the letters and journals?

Mailing a Letter

The United States Postal Service grew along with the United States. After the Louisiana Purchase, this government service expanded to the Rocky Mountains in 1803, and made it to the Pacific Coast in the 1840s. Forts such as Fort Kearney in Nebraska provided post offices, where pioneers could mail their letters. In 1815, a letter going less than 40 miles was 8 cents per sheet of paper. The price went up according to distance. Since 1863, the cost of postage has been based solely on weight.

CREATE A NEWSPAPER

Today, you might get your news from the Internet. For earlier generations, printed newspapers were the primary source for news. Some families back home received letters from people on the Oregon Trail, but you could also find the news from a newspaper.

❯ **In this activity,** you will create a typical newspaper that might have been seen during westward expansion. Research historical newspapers. A good resource is the Library of Congress at this site.

✶ What kind of news did newspapers provide?

✶ What was the style of writing?

✶ How were pages designed?

LOC chronicling America 🔎

❯ **Write down some of the more interesting headlines.** What makes them so interesting?

❯ **Make a timeline** of events between 1835 and 1862. Find information for this timeline in books and online.

✶ What was happening in the United States?

✶ What was happening in the rest of the world?

✶ How were the events connected?

❯ **Choose a date** within this time period. Create a newspaper with a page design, headlines, and articles that were typical for the period.

✶ What are your featured stories?

✶ Are there any cartoons or advertisements?

✶ How were newspapers then different from newspapers now?

CONSIDER THIS: Now, choose a page of a newspaper printed during the years of the Oregon Trail. How would you modernize it? Would you create a website? A Facebook page? How does the form of a published piece affect its content? How do you think we'll read our news in the future?

Chapter 4

LIFE ON THE TRAIL

Life on the Oregon Trail wasn't easy. Approximately 5 percent of people did not survive the journey. But there were also times of celebration. Romance on the trail led to weddings. Babies were born on the trail, too, and some were named after landmarks or seasons. When a mother didn't survive childbirth, another new mother would feed and care for the child.

The best way to travel the Oregon Trail was in a group. Experts recommended that groups have 50 to 70 armed men available to guard animals and protect against dangers. People formed groups based on relationships, geography, and interests.

? ESSENTIAL QUESTION

What were some of the necessities people needed when traveling west on the Oregon Trail?

epidemic: a disease that hits large groups at the same time and spreads quickly.

WORDS TO KNOW

A wagon train on the Oregon Trail was similar to a small county, with laws, rules, and even elections. There were penalties for stealing, gambling, and misbehavior. Pioneers made plans ahead of time for taking care of the sick and dividing their provisions in case of death.

INDEPENDENCE, MISSOURI

People started on the Oregon Trail from various places, depending on where they came from. Locations along the Missouri River were the most popular. Many people traveled to St. Louis and then took a steamboat up the Missouri River to a starting point.

No town was a more popular starting place than Independence, Missouri.

Beginning Towns on the Oregon Trail

Other towns saw their share of starts on the Oregon Trail, too. People already living in northern states and territories might start in Council Bluffs, Iowa. Some left from Fort Leavenworth in Kansas. People might leave from St. Joseph, Missouri, which would also become the birthplace of the Pony Express. When Independence, Missouri, was hit with a cholera **epidemic** in 1849, overlanders began choosing Westport, another town on the Missouri River. It had the added benefits of one fewer river crossing and one less day of travel on the trail. Today, Westport is downtown Kansas City, and Independence is one of the city's suburbs.

No matter where people started, they were usually on the same road by the time they reached Fort Kearny along the Platte River in Nebraska.

yoke: a wooden frame attached to the necks of work animals, such as oxen, to link them for towing or plowing.

WORDS TO KNOW

Missouri became a territory in 1812. William Clark served as territorial governor and built Fort Osage. Nearby, the town of Independence sat on the south bank of the Missouri River. Steam-powered riverboats regularly traveled from St. Louis, depositing travelers and supplies at the Independence landing. A mule-drawn train brought them the last few miles into town.

Independence was also the starting point for the Santa Fe Trail. In the early nineteenth century, the Santa Fe Trail took merchants and traders to Santa Fe, which was a part of Mexico at the time. Santa Fe, the oldest state capital city in North America, eventually became part of New Mexico.

Merchants realized Independence was a good place to set up business. They supplied traders on the Santa Fe Trail with whatever supplies and transportation they needed for the long journey. Later, they did the same for pioneers on the Oregon Trail. Main Street was almost always busy with people shopping.

DID YOU KNOW?

The future mayor of Independence, Robert Weston, built wagons for the overlanders. Weston marketed his wagons with the slogan, "A Weston Wagon Never Wears Out."

Wagons were the vehicle of choice on the Oregon Trail. Blacksmiths had a steady business converting farm wagons and shoeing animals.

In early spring, long lines of wagons started the journey from the Independence town square. An early start helped overlanders reach their final destination before winter. For most, it was the most difficult journey they would ever experience.

Hiram Young (1812–1883)

One Independence wagon maker was a former slave named Hiram Young. Born in Tennessee, he came to the Missouri Territory as a slave before earning his freedom. With his wife and daughter, Young moved to Independence in 1850. He began making wagons and ox **yokes** for overlanders. Hiram Young and Company become one of the largest businesses in Independence. The company was known for building wagons that could handle 6,000 pounds when pulled by 12 oxen.

Young was one of the most prosperous people in business. As the Civil War approached, tensions between free African Americans and whites in Missouri increased. Young and his family moved to Fort Leavenworth in Kansas until the war ended. After returning to Independence, Young was unable to achieve the same level of success he'd known before the war.

stamina: energy and strength to keep doing sometime for a period of time.

WORDS TO KNOW

WAGON TRAINS

The Oregon Trail was also demanding on the wagons and the animals that pulled them. Some wagons fell apart before the end of the journey.

Overlanders either modified farm wagons or purchased prairie schooners. Seasoned hardwood made the best wagons. The only springs were under the driver's seat. Many wagons didn't even have a driver's seat! It wasn't a comfortable ride, and belongings took up all the room.

Most people walked alongside the wagons with herds of sheep and cattle.

Pioneers had to think hard about which animals would pull their wagons. Horses, mules, or oxen? Horses were fast, but couldn't pull heavy loads as well as the other two. They also needed grain, which was heavy to haul. Mules had more **stamina**—they were able to travel up to 20 miles a day. Eight to ten mules pulling a 2,000-pound wagon was considered reasonable. But mules could be stubborn and hard to handle.

While mules traveled faster and weathered heat best, there were also advantages to oxen. They were more durable, could pull heavier loads, and weren't as picky about their grass. On a long trip such as the Oregon Trail, oxen were a popular choice.

About $25 for a pair of oxen was a good deal.
Four to six oxen walking side-by-side in pairs
could easily pull the typical wagon.

When families pulled up stakes to relocate in the Oregon Territory, they wanted to bring everything they owned. Rich travelers could send heavy items such as furniture, wood stoves, and pianos aboard ships that went around the tip of South America. Most people took their belongings on the wagon train, as well as all the supplies necessary for four to five months on the trail.

Many people overpacked. Their oxen wore out from the overwhelming loads. Plus, their wagons broke down or got stuck in mud because of the weight. Too much time was spent repairing and maintaining wagons.

> **DID YOU KNOW?**
>
> Most pioneers were farmers who brought seeds for planting and tools to work the land. The Oregon Territory was not developed enough to provide such things in stores.

U.S. Army Captain Randolph B. Marcy wrote about traveling with a group of New Yorkers to California on the trails.

"They were perfectly ignorant of every thing relating to this kind of campaigning, and had overloaded their wagons with almost every thing except the very articles most important and necessary; the consequence was, that they exhausted their teams, and were obliged to throw away the greater part of their loading. They soon learned that Champagne, East India sweetmeats, olives, etc., etc., were not the most useful articles for a prairie tour."

heirloom: a family possession handed down from generation to generation.

scurvy: a disease caused by lack of Vitamin C, with symptoms of weakness and bleeding gums.

WORDS TO KNOW

In order to make the trip, many people found out they had to lighten their loads. The Oregon Trail was littered with furniture, **heirlooms**, and other items owners had to say goodbye to if they wanted to complete the journey. These piles of things were referred to as "leeverites," because the pioneers had to "leave 'er right here."

FOOD FOR FUEL

Everyone had an idea about what to pack for the Oregon Trail. Some people looked to the opinion of experts who had made the trip before. A few early pioneers wrote handbooks that other people used to help them prepare for the journey ahead. Do you use travel books or travel websites when you plan a trip somewhere?

Although pioneers hoped to hunt and gather food along the way, there was always the chance that hunting wouldn't be successful. It wasn't guaranteed that you could kill enough food for an entire wagon train. Food supplies had to be items that would last and not spoil along the way, such as flour, sugar, coffee, and bacon.

DID YOU KNOW?

In later years, Mormon settlers on their way to Salt Lake Valley picked up the stuff that pioneers had discarded and sold the items to overlanders on their way to California.

Scurvy

Hippocrates, a physician from ancient Greece known as the "Father of Medicine," was the first to describe the disease of scurvy thousands of years ago. Left untreated, scurvy leads to bleeding and death. Sailors were particularly prone to scurvy until it was discovered that fresh fruit and vegetables—sources of Vitamin C—prevent scurvy.

For basic supplies, one person required about 15 pounds of coffee, 25 pounds each of bacon and sugar, and 100 pounds of flour. Flour and sugar were packed into sacks. Bacon could be cured and packed in barrels with bran to protect the bacon fat from melting. Dried vegetables and fruit were preferable to fresh ones to save space. Fruits and some vegetables (even pickles packed in vinegar) prevented **scurvy**.

Everyone drank coffee, even children! Water might taste bad along the trail, and the coffee helped mask the bad taste. Most families brought a milk cow or two along. A cow provided milk along the way and, in the case of a food shortage, it could be slaughtered for meat. Pioneers hung a barrel of cream from the wagon early in the day. The constant, bumpy movement churned the cream into fresh butter in time for dinner.

MORNING ON THE TRAIL

THE DAY PROGRESSES

THAT EVENING

WORDS TO KNOW

gutta percha: a tough, rubber-like material from tropical trees.

Dutch oven: a cooking pot that can be used over an open fire.

buckskin: deer hide.

chafe: to make sore with rubbing.

Every family needed camping equipment. People slept in tents or under wagons. Bedding was stored in bags made from **gutta percha**, or canvas, during the day. At night, the bag served as the bottom ground cloth.

Overlanders made soup or boiled meat in camp kettles. An extra camp kettle or gutta percha bag was used for gathering water. Cast iron pans, including **Dutch ovens**, were handy for frying and baking. Most people used tin cups and plates for meals. Wood wasn't as durable for camping supplies. Matches might have been the most important part of cooking equipment. Many a pioneer found their matches useless from getting dunked during a river crossing. Matches lasted longest when kept in bottles with tight corks.

DID YOU KNOW?

Gutta percha is a rigid, rubbery material from tropical trees. During the nineteenth century, it was used to make waterproof bags that would also float in water. Later, gutta percha began to be used as a filling material in dentistry.

PIONEER FASHION

Can you guess what the most important item of clothing was? If you guessed shoes, you are right! A pioneer could expect to wear out two pairs of shoes on the trail. People kept shoes until they could no longer be mended with pieces of leather or mule hide.

Wool clothing served as protection from rain, cold temperatures, and damage from the sun on the high plains. If you rode horses, you'd definitely want to reinforce the inside of your pants' inseam with **buckskin**. This made the pants last longer and reduced the amount of **chafing** on a rider's legs. It was a long way to ride with a rug burn on your thigh!

Pioneers were advised to bring along at least two changes of clothing, along with six pairs of socks, both wool and cotton. Wool sack coats kept people warm when they reached the snowy Rockies. Everyone wore hats and sunbonnets to protect them from the sun—this was in the days before sunscreen!

Don't think that just because you were on a wagon train traveling the Oregon Trail that you'd get out of brushing your teeth. Everyone packed toothbrushes, combs, and castile soap, which was used for cleaning almost everything, including teeth, body, and hair. Bar soap was used to keep clothes clean whenever the wagon train came to a river or other water source.

A TYPICAL DAY ON THE TRAIL

Harriet Scott wrote about heading off on the Oregon Trail.

"The first of April came—1852. The long line of covered wagons, so clean and white, but oh so battered, torn and dirty afterward: The loud callings and hilarity: many came to see us off. We took a last look at our dear homestead as it faded from our view."

The first days on the Oregon Trail were usually short. Constant walking over tough terrain was a new experience for both people and animals, and it was good to break the animals in gradually. After the animals were used to the routine, a good day of travel ranged from 15 to 20 miles in a day.

Landmarks on the Trail

Although the Oregon Trail was never a single trail, pieces of it were followed on foot, horseback, and wagon. Trails ran alongside rivers. A huge granite boulder that stood 128 feet high was reportedly named after an Independence Day celebration. Just west of Independence Rock was South Pass. Travelers rarely realized they had crossed the Continental Divide until they came to Pacific Springs and noticed the water traveling west instead of east.

WORDS TO KNOW

buffalo chips: the dried dung of buffalo, which burns easily.

sagebrush: a shrub that grows in the desert.

patriarch: the male leader of a family or group. A matriarch is the female leader.

Either a bugle or gunshot sounded at about 4 in the morning—time to get up! Women and children fixed a breakfast of bacon, Johnny cakes, and coffee while the men rounded up the livestock, which had been grazing and sleeping during the night. When breakfast was finished, everyone cleaned up, packed up, and hitched the animals to wagons.

Another blast around 7 a.m. signaled it was time for the wagon train to set off. Wagons driven by mules pulled out in front, since they moved faster than oxen. Unless you were sick or elderly, you walked.

But you weren't simply passing time, looking at the beautiful scenery. There were jobs to do as you went! Men on horses cleared the trail ahead, hunted for food, and herded the animals.

DID YOU KNOW?

Pioneers needed weapons for hunting and protection. The Hawken, Pennsylvania, and Kentucky rifles were popular, as were muskets.

**Women and children gathered edible plants
or scouted for fuel for the night's fires.**

The most popular fuel was **buffalo chips**. According to pioneer Enoch Conyers, women could "be seen roaming over the prairie with sacks in hand, searching for a few buffalo chips with their bare hands."

When the sun was highest in the sky, it was "nooning time," which meant stopping and taking a break. The animals were allowed to graze and rest. Pioneers dined on cold leftovers from the night before or food made during breakfast.

When the sun was no longer directly overhead, the animals were hitched back to the wagons and people continued on the trail, still doing chores. The wagon train came to rest for the night in late afternoon or early evening, when it chanced upon a spot with plenty of grass for grazing and water for people and animals to drink and bathe in.

At night, the wagons were parked in a circle for protection against wolves. Chores included caring for animals, preparing dinner, and setting up camp. Children even had schoolwork to do! Some pioneers might go fishing. If there wasn't enough wood or buffalo chips for evening fires, there was always **sagebrush**. After dinner, people relaxed. They played music, sang, danced, and told stories around the campfire, under the endless canopy of stars. Some people fell in love and got married, and these special events were celebrated with a party.

The Tucker Scott Family

The Tucker Scott family was one of many that traveled the Oregon Trail. They were headed by **patriarch** John Tucker Scott, who was born in Kentucky and grew up on the Illinois frontier. In 1852, he and his wife and several children made the journey. Only the three-year-old and five-year-old were free from assigned chores. Mary Francis, the oldest at 19, was the cook. The 17-year-old kept the family journal. A younger sister, Margaret Ann, aged 15, helped both her older sisters with their chores. Harvey, who was 14 years old, helped drive one of the wagons with help from his nine-year-old brother, John Henry. Catherine Amanda, 13, rode a horse and kept the herd in line.

Around 8 p.m., the wagon train settled down for the night. If the weather was nice, people slept under the stars. Otherwise, they slept in tents or under wagons. The first group of guards was on duty until midnight, when their replacements arrived.

Overlanders usually had the same routine day after day, except for Sundays. Wagon trains might spend part or all of Sundays on religious activities. If they were camped near clean water, Sundays were often laundry day.

CONQUERING NATURAL ELEMENTS

The Oregon Trail pioneers traveled over high plains, mountains, and deserts, through extreme heat and cold. The weather could turn in an instant to high winds or tornados and there was always the potential for thunderstorms, hail, and snow. Storms might wash out trails and soak everything you owned. Hail as big as oranges caused injuries, and once in a while, someone was struck by lightning. Dust was thick, causing problems for both people and animals.

Climate and weather can't be altered, so overlanders tried to be as prepared as possible. In the dry heat, they rubbed axle grease on their lips and fixed the cracked hooves of oxen with hot tar. Wood shrinks from the dryness of the desert, so at night, wagon wheels were left to soak in the rivers.

DID YOU KNOW?

Purifying the water was a constant chore. Locations such as the Platte River could be quite muddy. In 1852, Cecilia Adams wrote, "We can settle it with alum so that it is very good. Generally get a pint of mud out of every pail of water."

The trail followed rivers as much as possible to stay close to water. Wagon trains frequently crossed rivers, either by **fording** or ferry. Rivers might be swollen with rain or from melting snow, and rocks lay just beneath the surface. Some rivers had swift currents.

Wagons often overturned during a river crossing and belongings were lost—most people didn't know how to swim.

Fording Rivers

The journey to the West often meant dozens of river crossings. The best ways across rivers were ferries or fording at marked crossings. Ferries took wagons across a river for a small fee, but most often, pioneers were faced with fording. A ford is a shallow area of a river that can be crossed by wading, ideally getting only the wheels of a wagon wet. Gravel bars beneath the water surface created artificial bridges, but getting animals and wagons across a river was difficult. In some places, the water was so deep that animals were swept away by the current.

Other times, pioneers had to **caulk** their wagons to turn them into boats or move their belongings to actual boats, but even this was dangerous. The Applegate family made boats to float the Columbia River to The Dalles. They were hit by tragedy when a whirlpool sucked one of their rafts under.

ACCIDENTS AND DISEASE

What kinds of accidents do you have? Have you ever fallen out of a tree and broken your arm? Accidents were very common on the Oregon Trail. But there were no hospitals or doctors to visit when people got hurt. Getting run over by a wagon after slipping or falling from one were common accidents on the Oregon Trail. Many people were accidently shot. Others were caught in stampedes of animals.

Childbirth was particularly dangerous! The trail was a pretty dirty place, and there weren't many doctors or midwives. Plus, the wagon train would pause for only a short time while a woman gave birth. One woman wrote, "A few days later my eighth child was born. After this we picked up and ferried across the Columbia River, utilizing skiff, canoes, and flatboat to get across, taking three days to complete." That's a hard schedule for a mom and newborn baby!

Disease was another common killer on the Oregon Trail. Because overlanders lived close to each other and because they lacked the **immunizations** we have today, diseases such as tuberculosis, smallpox, measles, mumps, and flu spread quickly.

Pioneers did bring medicine kits on the trail, though they didn't look much like the first aid kits we have today. They contained pain-relieving medicines such as opium or laudanum, and quinine for malaria. Kits might contain castor oil for intestinal problems and hartshorn for snakebites. And if someone had a terrible stomach ache, they'd get peppermint oil.

Living in unsanitary conditions and drinking unpurified water meant frequent outbreaks of diseases such as cholera and dysentery.

┌─ ─ ─ ─ ─ ─ ─ ┐
│ **DID YOU KNOW?** │

│ From 1849 to 1853, cholera │
│ was the chief cause of │
│ death on the Oregon Trail. │
└─ ─ ─ ─ ─ ─ ─ ┘

A worldwide cholera **pandemic** originating in Asia struck during the nineteenth century. It most likely arrived in New Orleans and traveled up the Mississippi River to Missouri. Infected people then headed out on the Oregon Trail. Because of the large number of people on the trail, they might be exposed to cholera bacteria in garbage and the waters.

Pioneers on the Oregon Trail were no strangers to death. Overlanders built caskets from available wood and buried loved ones on the trail. The wagons packed the dirt down over the graves so that wolves or other wild animals wouldn't catch the scent.

Despite hardships, the travelers maintained their belief that a better life awaited them in the West. For many of them, their dreams did come true—they reached the far end of the trail.

ESSENTIAL QUESTION

Now it's time to consider and discuss the Essential Question: What were some of the necessities people needed when traveling west in the nineteenth century?

(PS)

Cholera's Reach

Harriet Scott lost her mother to cholera on the Oregon Trail. She described it.

"When we reached Wyoming, there in the Black Hills, this side of Ft. Laramie, the passing of that dear, beloved mother was a crushing blow to all our hopes. We had to journey on, and leave her in a lonely grave—a feather bed as a coffin, and the grave protected from the wolves by stones heaped upon it. The rolling hills were ablaze with beautiful wild roses—it was the 20th of June, and we heaped and covered mother's grave with the roses so the cruel stones were hid from view."

WATER PURIFICATION

IDEAS FOR SUPPLIES

2-liter bottles ✪ plastic cups ✪ pH testing strips ✪ scissors ✪ Italian salad dressing ✪ cheesecloth ✪ rubber band ✪ filtering materials, such as cotton balls, coffee filters, aquarium gravel, marbles

Water purification is just as important now as it was on the Oregon Trail. In towns and cities, most water is treated before it reaches your house. Have you ever gone camping? Did you have to purify your water? This activity will look at various ways water can be purified.

Caution: DO NOT drink experimentation water.

❯ **Research some of these ways to purify water.** What is involved with each method, and how easy would it be to do in the wild?

✱ Boiling

✱ Chemical treatment

✱ Commercial water filter, pumps, or gravity fed

✱ Commercial water purifiers, including ultraviolet

❯ **Design your own system.** Punch a hole near the top of the plastic cup to help with pressure during purification.

❯ **Cut the bottom off a 2-liter bottle.** Wrap a piece of cheesecloth around the mouth of the bottle, using a rubber band to secure it.

❯ **In a large, clean container,** mix five parts water to one part Italian salad dressing. This is your "gray water."

❯ **Using the pH testing strips,** test the water. It will probably test around 4. Anything below 7 is said to be acidic. Public water systems must have a pH level between 6.5 and 8.5.

❯ **Turn the 2-liter bottle over** so that it pours into the cup.

❯ **Choose a filter material** to place in the mouth of the bottle for your first layer. Pack the filtering layer so that it is 2 to 3 inches thick. Make sure your gray water is mixed, then pour a sample through the filter.

pH		
0	Sulfuric Acid (Battery Acid) (H2SO4)	
1	Stomach Acid	
2	Lemon Juice	Carbonated Beverages
3	Vinegar	
		Orange Juice
4	Tomatoes Acid Rain	Beer
5	Coffee	
	Pure Rain	Egg Yolks
6		
		Milk
7	Freshly Distilled Water, Saliva	Blood, Tears
8	Seawater Baking Soda (NaHCO3)	
9		
10		
11	Milk of Magnesia (Mg(OH)2)	
	Household Ammonia (NH3)	
12		
13	Household Bleach (NaClO)	
14	Lye (NaOH)	

Increasing acidity ∧ / Neutral / Increasing alkalinity ∨

Karen Balliet, Hans Kirkendoll

> **Test the pH** of the water in the plastic cup. Did it reach a normal level of 6.5 to 8.5? If the water is still acidic, add a second, different layer of another filtering material.

> **Pour another sample** of gray water and test the pH.

✱ Do you need to add a third layer of filtering?

CONSIDER THIS: Research water-borne diseases such as dysentery and cholera. How common are they? What protects us from these diseases today?

Historic Water Filters

When our ancestors first began filtering water, the main goal was to remove bugs and sediment or dirt from the water. One method was to lower barrels with holes drilled into the sides into muddy water. A bed of grass or moss in the barrel acted as a filter. People also placed handkerchiefs over cups of water to catch solids as they drank. Soon, they began boiling water to kill the contaminants that might cause cholera. Alum, charcoal, and the leaves of the prickly pear were also used to disinfect water.

DRYING FRUIT

Fruit is not only sweet and pleasant tasting, it also has vitamins that keep us healthy, such as Vitamin C. How long do you think fresh fruits such as apples lasted on the Oregon Trail? Probably not long! That's where drying came in. Drying fruit and meats meant these items wouldn't take up much space or spoil as quickly. You can dry your own fruit.

Caution: Ask an adult to help you cut the fruit.

❯ **Select fruit that is ripe** and free of bruises. Some good choices are:

* Apples
* Berries
* Bananas
* Peaches
* Pears

❯ **Wash the fruit, peel the skins,** and remove pits and cores. With a sharp knife, cut fruit in slices.

❯ **Preheat the oven to 170 degrees Fahrenheit.** Arrange fruit slices or whole berries in a single layer on a nonstick baking sheet without pieces touching. Place the baking sheet in the oven with the oven door slightly open.

❯ **Cook 4 to 8 hours until the fruit is dry.** Stir every 30 minutes. Remove from the oven and let sit out for about 12 hours. Store the dried fruit in storage bags or containers.

CONSIDER THIS: Do some research on how pioneers dried fruit in the nineteenth century. Compare the methods. Which one is faster and easier? Which one results in better-tasting fruit?

Dried Fruit for Dinner

Pioneers couldn't count on there being enough food on the trail, so they had to pack it. Since space was at a premium, desiccated fruit and vegetables were the best choice. Desiccating, or drying, is a way of removing the moisture from something. Today, commercial producers use special machines called dehydrators to remove the moisture from fruit. You can also use your oven at low heat. In the 1800s, people used the best heat and drying source they knew—the sun.

PACKING FOR A TRIP

Have you ever had to pack for a trip where space was limited?
Perhaps you could bring only a carry-on bag on an airplane or
a small bag for a car trip. How do you decide what to pack?

Planning was very important to people who traveled
on the Oregon Trail. It might mean the difference
between success and failure. This activity will show you
the importance of planning and decision making.

❭ **Plan a 100-mile bicycle trip** using only what you can carry with you.

✱ What is your destination?

✱ How far will you travel each day?

✱ Where will you sleep?

✱ How will you transport your supplies for the trip?

❭ **Begin a packing list.** What will you bring for:

✱ Clothing

✱ Food

✱ Camping/cooking supplies

❭ **Try to imagine emergency scenarios.** Make a list of dangerous things
that might happen during your trip. What do you need to bring to be safe?

CONSIDER THIS: What does the length of the trip mean for your packing?
What about your destination? What can you do in today's world that you
couldn't do on the Oregon Trail?

DID YOU KNOW?

Randolph B. Marcy's book, *The Prairie Traveler: A Hand-Book for Overland Expeditions*, had seven chapters covering everything the pioneer should know, from handling trail animals to hunting wild animals. Supplies for the trail were covered in the first chapter. They could be summed up as food, clothing, and weapons.

MAKING MOCCASINS

How long do you think your shoes would last on the Oregon Trail? Today, experts suggest replacing shoes after 500 miles. If you were to take this advice, you would need four or five pairs of shoes for the Oregon Trail!

Most pioneers had two pairs of shoes, and they often wore out before the end of the trail. Pioneers tried to make them last by patching them with leather or animal hide. But at some point, many people found themselves either trading for or making moccasins similar to those that Native Americans wore.

This activity will allow you to make a pair of shoes from common items found around the house.

❯ **Decide on the materials** you want to use. Some ideas are leftover cloth, old canvas bags, felt, paper for patterns, pins, needle and thread.

❯ **Spread some paper** on the ground and step on it. Lightly mark around your feet with a pencil before stepping off. This is your pattern.

❯ **With a ruler,** measure and mark about 4 to 5 inches larger than the outline of your foot. This is your cutting line.

❯ **Cut out the pattern** and pin it to your shoe material. Cut out the material. You can remove the pattern afterwards.

❯ **Bend the shoe shape in half** the long way. Sew one edge of the shoe closed. This will be your heel.

❯ **Try on the shoe.** Carefully, pin the material closed over the top of your foot. Leave enough room so that you can take your shoe on and off.

❯ **Remove the shoe and sew** along the top where you have placed the pins. Cut off the excess material.

❯ **Turn your moccasin inside out.** Repeat all the steps for your other foot. You now have a new pair of shoes!

CONSIDER THIS: Native Americans often decorated their moccasins. What kind of decorations might you use on your moccasins? What would those decorations mean?

Chapter 5

THE END OF THE TRAIL

Travel on the Oregon Trail became easier as time passed, simply because of the number of people who traveled it. Thousands of wagons packed down the trail so that it became more like a road. People discovered shortcuts and landmarks became familiar because of letters from pioneers and newspaper accounts.

Trading posts, military forts, or sometimes a combination of the two began appearing near the trail. These were like rest stops where people could buy supplies and make repairs. The U.S. Army built forts and camps along the Oregon Trail to help establish order for both overlanders and Native Americans. Most of these forts were used only briefly for protection or as supply stations.

? ESSENTIAL QUESTION

What was the effect of the Oregon Trail on Native American history?

Later pioneers shared the Oregon Trail with riders on the Pony Express, who delivered mail, or stagecoaches that began expanding their routes. The Oregon Trail had become an important road for the United States.

LANDMARKS ALONG THE OREGON TRAIL

When people traveled on the Oregon Trail, they were introduced to geographical regions and natural landmarks they had never seen before. The Great Plains was like a huge sea of grass. Beyond it were the Rocky Mountains, extending as far north and south as the Great Plains.

On the other side of the Rockies was the Great Basin, a dry area with deserts to the south. More mountains appeared on the other side of the basin, the Sierra Nevadas to the south and the Cascade and Blue Mountains in the northwest. In the Blue Mountains, visitors could see trees 200 feet high. Waterfalls could be heard from long distances. And finally, the rugged coastline of the Pacific Ocean, so very different from the Atlantic coast.

Fort Kearny

A series of long, low buildings with flat roofs located near the Platte River was a welcome site for the pioneers. This was Fort Kearny, built on land bought from the Pawnee for the protection of the pioneers on the trail. Buildings built from **adobe** and **sod** were located where several trails came together from Independence, Omaha, and Council Bluffs. Fort Kearny was a major stop for soldiers, pioneers, suppliers, and the Pony Express. Overlanders often sent mail to friends and family in the East from Fort Kearny, knowing that it might be a long time before they had the opportunity again.

Register Cliff was a popular location for pioneers to inscribe their names. (Gates Frontiers Fund Wyoming Collection within the Carol M. Highsmith Archive, Library of Congress, Prints and Photographs Division)

Some landmarks, such as Register Cliff and Independence Rock, were like message boards. People left their names and dates on the rocks. Carving or writing on landmarks is no longer allowed—today, we want to protect the history of those landmarks.

NATIVE AMERICANS ON THE OREGON TRAIL

Explorers and pioneers were not the first people to see the beauty of the American West. Native Americans lived there long before Europeans arrived. As more and more white people spread across more and more of the land, Native Americans struggled to keep the land where they had always lived. Sometimes, this struggle led to conflict and violence.

Between 1840 and 1860, 362 pioneers on the trail were killed by Native Americans. This number is smaller than the number of Native Americans killed by pioneers—426. The threat of an attack was greatest on the west side of South Pass, along the Snake and Humboldt Rivers. The worst attack on the Oregon Trail occurred in Murphy, Idaho, when the Utter wagon train suffered 11 deaths. Pioneers killed 25 Native Americans.

Many Native American tribes lived in the West, particularly Plains tribes such as the Lakota, Crow, and Blackfeet. Remember Sacagawea, who was part of the Lewis and Clark Expedition? Her people, the Shoshone, and the Nez Perce also lived close to the Oregon Trail. Other Native American tribes lived along the Pacific coast.

Many Native Americans were not aggressive. Some approached the wagon trains out of curiosity, as Jesse Berryman Jones described.

"We had stopped for our noon meal when there came riding about a hundred painted warriors . . . father gave the chief some bread and milk."

According to Jones, the head warrior returned the milk after tasting it, but approved of the bread and shared it with others in his party.

Other tribes were more interested in trading. They brought moccasins and buffalo robes to trade for knives, food, and other items from overlanders.

The Native Americans were known to help starving pioneers or return lost children. Inez Parker recalled her mother setting her nine-month-old sister in an open spot out of the way while the men worked on getting a wagon down from a mountain. When the mother checked on her daughter, she saw a group of Indians on horses where she had left her baby. The mother ran over, ready to defend her daughter, only to find that the Native Americans had circled the child to protect her until her mother's return.

DID YOU KNOW?

The greatest danger from Native Americans was horse thievery. In some tribes, stealing a good horse or a number of horses was considered an honor.

Westward expansion had a devastating effect on the way of life of Native Americans. Settlers brought diseases such as smallpox and measles, which Native Americans had no resistance to. Some tribes experienced large numbers of deaths from these diseases.

For Native Americans, the river of white people never stopped. Buffalo and wild game began to disappear from overhunting. Eventually, the federal government and settlers would want the land on either side of the Oregon Trail as well.

As more and more settlers arrived, the Native Americans were squeezed onto ever-shrinking parcels of land. Some tribes fought against the pioneers and soldiers, while others tried to find peaceful solutions. When the transcontinental railroad was built and more towns and territories were established, the federal government solved what it saw as the "problem" of Native Americans by taking their land and forcing them to move to **reservations**.

exile: banished from living in a certain place.

livelihood: a source of income.

extinction: when a species dies out and there are no more left in the world.

conservation: managing and protecting natural resources.

WORDS TO KNOW

WE SHALL DIE NO MORE FOREVER

One of the most respected of the peaceful resisters was Chief Joseph (1840–1904) of the Nez Perce. In the 1870s, Chief Joseph refused to move his band from Oregon Country to a small reservation in Idaho at the demand of the federal government, which wanted access to the gold found on the land. Even after Chief Joseph and his tribe reluctantly agreed to be moved, they were pursued by the U.S. Army. Although opposed to war, Joseph joined his people in battle.

A band of about 700 Nez Perce held off 2,000 U.S. soldiers in numerous battles, earning grudging respect from military leader General William Tecumseh Sherman. But Chief Joseph knew surrender was the only option. He formally surrendered on October 5, 1877. He gave the following speech.

"It is cold, and we have no blankets. The little children are freezing to death. My people, some of them, have run away to the hills, and have no blankets, no food. No one knows where they are—perhaps freezing to death. I want to have time to look for my children, and see how many of them I can find. Maybe I shall find them among the dead. Hear me, my chiefs! I am tired. My heart is sick and sad. From where the sun now stands I will fight no more forever."

Chief Joseph died in **exile** in 1904.

Chief Joseph, Nez Perce
(National Archives)

WHERE THE BUFFALO ROAM

When the earliest pioneers began traveling the Oregon Trail, they saw huge shaggy beasts that weighed up to 2,000 pounds. Diary entries tell of problems with stampedes or wandering bulls entering camp. They were American bison, commonly referred to as buffalo because they resembled Asian buffalo. About 200 to 300 million buffalo lived on the Great Plains, and the Plains tribes depended on them for their **livelihood**.

Because Native Americans used every part of an animal, and took only as many as they needed, there were plenty of buffalo on the plains. Buffalo provided meat, clothing, leather, sinew to use in bows, hooves to make glue, and dried droppings for fires. When commercial hunters began to hunt large numbers of buffalo for sport and for hides, they'd leave the rest of the animal to rot where it lay. By the mid-1800s, almost 100,000 buffalo robes were being traded every year.

When the transcontinental railroad was being built, much of the remaining buffalo fed railway workers and soldiers at the forts. In 1884, it was estimated that only 325 wild buffalo remained in the United States. The buffalo faced **extinction**. Today, because of **conservation** efforts, these protected herds number approximately 30,000.

American bison (Agricultural Resource Service)

moderate: a reasonable or medium amount.

CALIFORNIA GOLD

Not everyone on the Oregon Trail was heading to the Oregon Territory. Some went as far as Fort Hall in Idaho and took a turn for California. In the early years, travelers on the Oregon Trail were often families looking for fresh starts as farmers or merchants. That all changed after a man named James Marshall (1810–1885) migrated to California and began overseeing the construction of a sawmill on the American River.

On January 24, 1848, at Sutter's Mill, Marshall spied flecks of gold in the mud.

Although people tried to keep it secret, it was a secret that couldn't be kept. Oregonians heard about it when a group of people tried to buy all available mining supplies from Fort Vancouver. By August 1848, the discovery of gold in California had made headlines in newspapers throughout the world. Stories spread of people who made it rich. Tens of thousands of goldseekers poured onto the California Trail.

A fork in the trail lay just beyond Fort Hall, which had been established in 1834 by fur trader Nathaniel Wyeth before being sold to Hudson's Bay Company. On one side was a sign that said, "To Oregon." On the other path was a pile of gold-colored rocks. These rocks marked the way to California. Starting in 1849, large numbers of people chose California. Unlike the pioneer families of earlier years, many of these travelers were single men or men who had left their families to make their fortune in gold.

By the time many of these miners made it to California, not much gold remained. Some found **moderate** success. Many moved to other areas to try their luck. Some became ranchers, farmers, or shopkeepers. Others turned around and followed the trail back home.

THE END OF THE TRAIL

For the many pioneers traveling to the Oregon Territory, the trail stopped at The Dalles, named by French-Canadian trappers. In French, *dalles* means "the river rapids through a narrow gorge." Pioneers often traded in their wagons for canoes, or they built large rafts for the wagons to float down to Willamette Valley, the final destination for most people. The Whitmans established their mission, called Wascopam, there in 1838.

> ### DID YOU KNOW?
>
> Lewis and Clark camped at The Dalles in April 1806 and watched nearby tribes catching salmon with nets and spears.

In 1845, the Barlow family arrived at The Dalles to find no boats available. Samuel Barlow began looking for another way to the Willamette Valley. He discovered an Indian trail south of the Columbia River and around Mount Hood.

Barlow and Phillip Foster went into business by building the Mount Hood Toll Road. Travelers were charged a toll to use this road, later known as Barlow Road. Within a year of being built, this road would be traveled by more than half of the overlanders on the way to Willamette Valley.

Willamette Valley was a fertile valley that had good soil, plenty of water, and a good climate for crops. Oregon City was established in the valley by John McLoughlin in 1842. Within two years, it had a newspaper, a variety of businesses, and a land claims office.

half-breed: a term, now considered offensive, meaning the offspring of parents of different races.

WORDS TO KNOW

Waterfalls provided power for the nearby mills. Soon, Oregon City became the center of government and the capital of the Oregon Territory. Newly arrived pioneers camped in Oregon City while filing land claims.

HOMESTEADING

In 1841, Senator Lewis Linn of Missouri introduced a bill to Congress offering free land in Oregon to white settlers and "**half-breed**" Native Americans. His reason for specifying half-breed was to include only the offspring of white males and Native American wives and to exclude all other people of color. The bill didn't pass, but Senator Linn continued to introduce the bill every year until it did pass nine years later.

The Donation Land Act became law in 1850. It provided 640 acres of farmland to married couples already living in Oregon and half that amount to single settlers. Those arriving after the passage of the Donation Act received 160 acres if single or 320 acres if married. In the rest of the United States, people had to pay $200 for 160 acres. In the Oregon Territory, that much land was free as long as you were at least 18 years old.

The land office issued 7,437 land patents under the Donation Land Act. By 1854, land in Oregon was being sold at $1.25 an acre, with claims limited to 320 acres.

The U.S. government passed the Homestead Act of 1862 with the primary purpose of encouraging settlement in the Great Plains, but the act included Oregon. The cost for the land? A $34 filing fee.

Approximately 17 percent of the state was settled through homesteading. The amount of land was the same as for people who arrived after passage of the Donation Act—160 acres. The only requirements for homesteading was that the land must be lived on and farmed for five years. More than 1.6 million people took advantage of this opportunity, including women over the age of 21. Four women were among the first to file for homesteads.

The Homestead Act encouraged settlement by allowing any U.S. citizen the opportunity to own land. It resulted in a settlement boom for the West as schools, businesses, and communities developed.

DID YOU KNOW?

The town of Beatrice, Nebraska, passed a Homestead Act in 2010. Applicants received free land with the conditions that they build a house on it within a year and live in it for three years.

91

BECOMING A STATE

Although the Oregon Territory was located far from the battlegrounds where the Civil War would soon be fought, its future was still affected by the issue of slavery. Politicians wanted to know whether Oregon would be a free state or a slave state before it was admitted to the Union.

The people of the Oregon Territory held a constitutional convention in the summer of 1857 to draft a state constitution and to make some decisions about the future. The capital had moved to Salem, where delegates met to form a constitution modeled after other farming states, such as Iowa and Indiana.

In the fall, Oregonians voted on three questions.

- Did they approve of the new Oregon Constitution?

- Should slavery be allowed in Oregon?

- Should African Americans be allowed to live in Oregon outside of slavery?

The only question that voters said "yes" to was in adopting the new constitution.

Slavery wouldn't be allowed, but neither would African-American residents. By the next summer, voters elected the officials identified in the territorial constitution. Residents now just had to wait while the federal government debated whether to admit the free state of Oregon. It finally came to a vote, and on February 14, 1859, President James Buchanan signed the bill admitting Oregon to the United States of America.

ESSENTIAL QUESTION

Now it's time to consider and discuss the Essential Question: What was the effect of the Oregon Trail on Native American history?

HOMESTEADING

In 1850, the Donation Land Act was passed, and 12 years later, the Homestead Act of 1862 was passed. Both acts gave away land. Homesteading was settling a piece of land by living on it. In U.S. history, these were often farms.

This activity explores nineteenth-century homesteading and its role in westward expansion.

❯ **Read the Donation Land Act** and the Homesteading Act of 1862 here. You can find the full texts at these sites.

Donation Land Act 🔍

Homestead Act 🔍

❯ **Compare and contrast** the two documents and answer the following questions.

* Which parts are similar?

* What is different about the documents?

* Why was the government giving away land? What is the purpose of homesteading? Can you find other examples of the government encouraging homesteading?

❯ **Create a way to present your research.** Will you create a chart, a diagram, or a PowerPoint presentation? Consider the needs of your audience. What is the best way to show your information?

CONSIDER THIS: Not everyone was in favor of homesteading. Many Northern factory owners worried about losing workers. Southern plantation owners often worried that small farms in the West would be against the slavery that plantations depended on for labor. Can you think of any other potential problems with homestead acts?

The first homestead under the 1862 Homestead Act (Library of Congress)

GRAFFITI

When pioneers carved their names and dates on rocks and cliff walls along the Oregon Trail, they were recording their existence at specific dates and times. They were also leaving this information in a public place for everyone to see.

If you were to leave your name, date, and other information in a public location today, it might be considered graffiti. It might also get you arrested! Why is what pioneers did 150 years ago illegal today?

Independence Rock has been called the "Register of the Desert." What is a register, and what uses did it have then? Are there any uses for a register now?

❭ **Define graffiti.**

✱ What is the purpose of graffiti?

✱ Is graffiti the same as defacing public property? Why or why not?

✱ Does graffiti communicate? How?

❭ **Look for modern examples** of graffiti in the news or in your community.

❭ **With your friends,** create a graffiti wall using large sheets of paper. Don't write on walls or other permanent surfaces!

❭ **Using art supplies,** write or draw messages on the graffiti wall that might come from someone your age on the Oregon Trail.

CONSIDER THIS: Some people argue that graffiti is art? What do you think?

Graffiti as Art

Chances are that you've seen negative press about graffiti, but more and more public facilities and businesses are finding that graffiti brings positive attention. Professional graffiti artists, also known as street or urban artists, have been hired to cover large sections of walls. For example, the Canada Science and Technology Museum held a graffiti contest to cover the walls surrounding its construction site in 2016.

BUILD A FORT

No matter where pioneers started, what shortcuts they took, or where they ended their journey, one thing was for certain—they passed trading post forts, some active and some abandoned. Some were filled with soldiers, while others resembled a country store. Forts were a place to get news, supplies, and assistance.

In this activity, you will learn about the roles of forts and trading posts in settling the West.

❯ **When you read the word "fort,"** what do you think of? If you think of stockade fences made of logs, you're not alone. But not all forts were built in this style.

❯ **Research forts of the American West.** Search by individual fort names. Many historical societies, museums, and state tourism agencies also provide information about forts. These websites are also possible resources.

Plains frontier forts 🔍

trading post forts 🔍

❯ **Once you have done some research,** answer the following questions.

✱ What types of materials were used to make forts?

✱ What were the advantages and disadvantages of the building materials used?

✱ Did the fort have a single purpose or many purposes? What were they?

✱ Who were the primary occupants of the fort?

❯ **Choose one to build a model of.** What would be the best way to show the fort? What is the audience that you want to reach?

CONSIDER THIS: Compare and contrast Western forts to earlier forts built east of the Mississippi River. Do they look the same? Was the function and purpose of the forts the same?

DID YOU KNOW?

The U.S. government bought Fort John in 1849 and renamed it Fort Laramie. Buildings were added until they numbered 180. Fort Laramie was the largest military fort in the West and a stop for the Pony Express and Overland Stage.

THROUGH THE EYES OF A NATIVE AMERICAN TEEN

Estimates of Native Americans in the United States before the arrival of Europeans range from 1.8 to 18 million people, according to the Smithsonian National Museum of the American Indian. Native American populations reached their lowest level during the nineteenth century—about 250,000. They died of disease, war, and limited resources, while white Americans took over the land that was once theirs.

❯ **Imagine that you are a Native American teenager** living in the northwestern United States in 1840. You have heard about covered wagons and white people traveling across the Great Plains. What do you think of this news? Does it frighten you or make you excited? How do you imagine your life will change from meeting white people? Will it change for the better or for the worse?

❯ **Write a diary entry from the perspective** of a Native American teenager in 1840. Be sure to include your feelings and concerns about the future.

❯ **Write another diary entry from the point of view** of a Native American in 1860. Are the feelings and concerns different from what they were in 1840? Why or why not?

CONSIDER THIS: By the time the period of westward expansion on the Oregon Trail ended, the federal government was removing Native American children from their families and placing them in boarding schools. Some children in these schools kept diaries. Read some of the entries at this website. Do you think white people were right to send Native American children away to boarding school? Why or why not?

PBS Indian boarding schools 🔍

DID YOU KNOW?

A measles outbreak among the Cayuse tribe led to an attack on the Whitman Mission in 1847. Among the Cayuse, a doctor's life was forfeited if a patient died. The Cayuse blamed the Whitmans for the deaths of their children from measles, and killed more than a dozen of the settlers.

Chapter 6

THE TRANSCONTINENTAL
RAILROAD

If you were to take a trip across the United States today, how would you go? By plane? By car? You might get to make the journey by train. During the time of the Oregon Trail, this wasn't an option—there was no train that stretched across the entire country.

On July 1, 1862, President Abraham Lincoln signed the Pacific Railway Act. This act united the federal government and private railway companies with a common goal—a railroad from one end of the continent to another. Building the Transcontinental Railroad was expected to take up to 10 years, and everyone believed it would change life in the United States.

? ESSENTIAL QUESTION

What are some ways the Transcontinental Railroad changed life in the United States?

WORDS TO KNOW

steam engine: an engine that burns wood or coal to heat water and create steam. The steam generates power to run the engine.

Industrial Revolution: the name of the period of time that started in England in the late 1700s when people started using machines to make things in large factories.

Isthmus of Panama: a narrow strip of land between the Caribbean Sea and the Pacific Ocean in Central America.

THE RAILROAD HEADS WEST

The **steam engine** was first introduced during the eighteenth-century **Industrial Revolution** in Great Britain. It made its way to the United States by 1830 and was greeted with both excitement and suspicion. Within 10 years, almost 3,000 miles of track had been laid east of the Mississippi River. Railways, powered by steam engines, connected cities and provided a better way to transport goods.

Meanwhile, those cities were becoming crowded as large numbers of immigrants came to the United States to find a better life for themselves and their families. As more and more people made the long and hazardous trip across the country on the Oregon Trail, many wondered if there was a better way to get there.

At the same time that gold was being discovered in California, the United States was ending its war with Mexico.

DID YOU KNOW?

Merchants, pioneers, and miners wanted a faster way to the West Coast that didn't involve sailing around Cape Horn on the tip of South America or risking tropical diseases from crossing the **Isthmus of Panama**.

With the Treaty of Guadalupe Hidalgo, the United States expanded once more by adding the land from Texas to California. More than ever, people wanted to explore and settle the West. And now, the United States had a way to make it happen faster—the railroad.

The government began to explore options for a transcontinental railroad even before President Lincoln was elected. In 1853, Secretary of War Jefferson Davis had ordered surveyors to find the best route. Six survey teams recommended six different routes! It became a political debate, with Southern politicians wanting a southern route and Northern politicians wanting a northern route.

National Parks

The Oregon Trail is an important part of U.S. history. In 1978, Congress established the Oregon National Historic Trail in recognition of its significance. The protected path includes trails with the original wagon ruts plus routes now covered by roads. Part of the National Trails System, the Oregon National Historic Trail travels across more than 125 historic sites. It is administered by the National Park Service and managed by many groups, including the Bureau of Land management, Forestry Services, private and tribal landowners, and state governments. You can see images of some of these sites on an interactive map at the National Park Service website.

NPS Oregon places to go 🔍

President Lincoln grew up on the frontier just west of the Mississippi River. He knew how hard it was to travel long distances by horseback. After two years in office, he signed the Pacific Railway Act, which called for a railway at the 32nd parallel. This was the shortest route. A **telegraph** line would also be built along the railroad. The government would use the telegraph and the railroad to deliver messages, mail, and the military to the West.

THE FIRST TRANSCONTINENTAL RAILROAD

The federal government chose two railway companies to build the railroad. The newly formed Union Pacific would lay track west from Omaha, Nebraska. The established Central Pacific would build toward the east from Sacramento, California.

The cost of building a transcontinental railroad would be high. The government gave 170 million acres to the railroad. For every mile of track laid, the companies received a square mile of public land to sell to future settlers. Since **incentives** came from the number of miles of track built, the race was on for each company to build more faster.

The Union Pacific Railway had to construct several trestles over gaps for the Transcontinental Railroad. (Library of Congress)

The Central Pacific gained ground early because of a large population of Chinese immigrants who worked very hard. The **terrain** of the Sierra Nevada Mountains proved to be especially difficult for the railroad workers. They had to tunnel through granite mountains! But Central Pacific work crews finally made it through California and Nevada.

The Union Pacific started much later, first laying track in Nebraska to connect to the eastern U.S. rail network on December 2, 1863. In many places, these tracks lay near the Oregon Trail. In slightly more than two years, the Union Pacific built 140 miles of track on a route that required the track to cross deep ravines.

By this time, the Civil War was raging and men who might have been available to work on the tracks were caught up in fighting. The war also affected the availability of supplies.

Construction picked up once the Civil War ended and the Union Pacific lay track across the easier plains of Nebraska and the southern border of Wyoming.

Both companies raced to the finish—the meeting point was set at Promontory Summit in Utah. The final spike—a golden spike—was driven into the ground on May 10, 1869, three years ahead of schedule. The next day, the first transcontinental train brought freight from California to the East Coast. The first passenger service began May 15.

The laying of the golden spike. Samuel S. Montague, from Central Pacific Railroad, shakes hands with Grenville M. Dodge, from Union Pacific Railroad. (Andrew J. Russell)

When the railroad was finished, a telegraph was sent to the East with one word: "Done."

What had been a grueling, six-month trip by foot to California now took only two weeks. And within only a few years, the Transcontinental Railroad transformed the frontier wilderness. The country filled with towns, homesteads, and increasing numbers of American settlers and growing industries.

RAILWAYS TO THE PACIFIC NORTHWEST

Once the Transcontinental Railroad was complete, pioneers taking the train to Oregon still had to get off at certain stops, including Cheyenne, Wyoming, or Salt Lake City, Utah, and travel overland to reach locations in the Pacific Northwest. Within 14 years, that too changed.

The Oregon & California Railroad connected Sacramento to Oregon. Another railway, the Oregon Short Line, offered train passengers a direct route to Oregon from the transcontinental railway stop in Granger, Wyoming.

In 1870, construction began on the Northern Pacific Railway, a northern transcontinental route across the United States from Chicago through Wisconsin, North Dakota, Montana, Idaho, and Oregon, ending at Puget Sound in Washington. Like the first transcontinental railroad, this northern route was a challenge to build. It had to be laid across the Badlands of North Dakota. The rugged land got its name from the Lakota, who knew how lack of water and extreme temperatures made travel there difficult.

The Northern Pacific Railway also had to cross the Continental Divide in Montana, just as Lewis and Clark had done so long ago. But, unlike Lewis and Clark, who traveled south along the Snake River, the Northern Pacific Railway continued traveling north and west across the Cascades Mountains to reach the Pacific Ocean. Construction of the Northern Pacific Railway was completed on September 7, 1883, with another gold spike in Gold Creek, Montana.

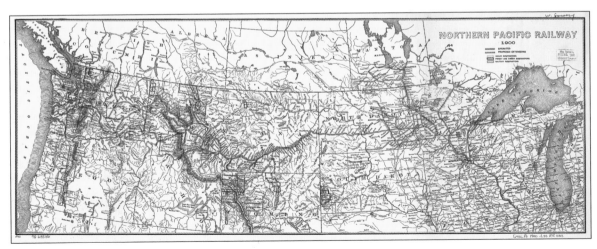

The Northern Pacific Railroad around the 1900s (Library of Congress)

sabotage: to deliberately damage or destroy.

derailment: when a train runs off the rails of a track.

lucrative: something that is profitable, that makes money.

revenue: income or earnings.

boom town: a town that has tremendous and quick growth.

WORDS TO KNOW

RESERVATIONS

Not everyone benefitted from the railroad. By the time tracks were being laid, most Plains tribes could see that things were getting worse. More white people meant less land for Native Americans. Some tribes attacked survey and work crews. Others attempted to **sabotage** the actual iron rails by destroying track or causing **derailments**.

After the Civil War ended, the government posted more military in the West. The Transcontinental Railroad was a priority, so moving the Plains tribes became a top task for the U.S. Army. Territories and towns sprang up around the railroad, pushing Native Americans off lands where they had lived and hunted for centuries. Previous treaties made with the federal government were not honored if gold or good farmland was found on Indian lands.

Train Robberies

The Transcontinental Railroad was appreciated by groups other than railroad executives and settlers. It also provided new opportunities for outlaws, such as Butch Cassidy and his Wild Bunch. On June 2, 1899, Cassidy and his gang held up the Union Pacific train near Wilcox, Wyoming, robbing passengers and breaking open the safe with dynamite. The safe held gold to pay troops in the Spanish-American War. Butch Cassidy's daring train robbery made national news. It wouldn't be his last train robbery, but it was perhaps the most **lucrative** one.

Butch Cassidy and the Wild Bunch, 1900

For a time, Native Americans fought back. But events such as the Sand Creek massacre, when as many as 160 Native Americans, including women and children, were killed, took their toll. The near extinction of the buffalo was devastating to the Native American population.

By the end of the 1800s, almost 300,000 Native Americans had been forced to leave their homelands and move to reservations.

RAILROAD TOWNS

Years of heavy traffic on the Oregon Trail had led to the establishment of many small communities along the way. Those communities celebrated the news of the construction of the railroads. Railroads meant growth and **revenue**.

The railways gave birth to new towns and territories, including Montana Territory and Dakota Territory. The Wyoming Territory was reorganized when parts of Utah and Idaho were added to it. Railway towns became **boom towns**.

The Northern Pacific Railway traveled through forested areas. Timber companies prospered as they provided the wood for railroad ties, mine shafts, and the expansion of towns. Merchants provided goods for the railroad workers. People turned their homes into boarding houses for the people who were flocking to the new towns and territories to find work and prosperity.

Others were hired to work construction on the railroad. There were many opportunities to make money as the railroads expanded.

Even those locations that were not suitable for farming or mining benefitted from **industrialization** and trade because of the railroads. For example, General Grenville M. Dodge and his survey crew plotted a site for a new town on July 5, 1867. Four months later, tracks of the first transcontinental railway reached this new town, which was named Cheyenne. Soon, Cheyenne's population surged to 4,000 people. In early 1888, the Union Pacific board of directors decided Cheyenne would be a major **depot** on the Transcontinental Railroad.

Mark Twain in the West

"At 4.20 P.M., Sunday, we rolled out of the station at Omaha, and started westward on our long jaunt. A couple of hours out, dinner was announced —an 'event' to those of us who had yet to experience what it is to eat in one of Pullman's hotels on wheels . . . ."

The West appealed to writers such as Mark Twain, whose real name was Samuel Langhorne Clemens (1835–1910). Twain had journeyed west in 1861 in a stagecoach. He later made the trip again, by train. He describes his journeys and time spent in the West in his 1872 book, *Roughing It.* You can read the book and look at the illustrations at this website.

Mark Twain Roughing It 🔍

(Doug Letterman)

The Transcontinental Railroad united America in a way that settlement alone could not. American society became more mobile and industrialized. The railroad also served as the beginning of the end of the Oregon Trail. Why go through the danger and hardships of traveling by wagon and foot when there was a faster, easier way to travel west? Some people continued to use the Oregon Trail for a while longer, but eventually, all that was left were faint wagon tracks in the dirt.

The Oregon Trail served a very important purpose by providing new opportunities to half a million people. The United States prospered and grew because of the Oregon Trail, which could be seen as a symbol of the human urge to explore, to conquer, and to take a chance for a better life. What about you? If you had lived in the mid-1800s, would you have packed up all you could carry in a wagon and headed west?

ESSENTIAL QUESTION

Now it's time to consider and discuss the Essential Question: What are some ways the Transcontinental Railroad changed life in the United States?

WHERE DO YOU COME FROM?

How much do you know about your nineteenth-century ancestors? One of the most interesting facts about most Americans is that, unless you're Native American, everyone has ancestors who originated from somewhere else. The United States was largely founded by immigrants. This activity will get you started on your family's history in the United States.

❯ **Look at** *The New York Times* **Immigration Explorer** at this website and click on the earliest year, 1880.

NYT Immigration Explorer 🔍

✱ What does the interactive map tell you about areas settled largely from the Oregon Trail?

❯ **Click on the part of the country** where you currently live. Where did people who settled your region originally come from?

❯ **Look at immigration data** for 1820–1869 here.

✱ What are the total number of immigrants for the time period?

✱ What countries did they come from?

Scholastic immigration data 🔍

❯ **Create a way to present your research.** Will you create a chart, a diagram, or a PowerPoint presentation? Consider the needs of your audience. What is the best way to show your information?

CONSIDER THIS: Do you have an ancestor who was an emigrant who traveled one of the trails west, such as the Oregon Trail? Provide information about their travels to the Oregon-California Trails Association at this website and you might receive your own emigrant certificate.

Oregon paper trail 🔍

Modern Kids on the Oregon Trail

During the summer of 2008, 24 students left their homes in the city for a two-week journey by wagon train on the Oregon Trail. They exchanged shorts and T-shirts for pioneer clothing. The group traveled by horse and mule-drawn wagons. They slept in tents and cooked outdoors. You can learn more about their adventures in the video, *In Pursuit of a Dream*, produced by Boston Productions Inc., in cooperation with the Oregon-California Trails Association.

In Pursuit of a Dream video 🔍

REPORTING ON THE TRANSCONTINENTAL RAILROAD

"The crowd cheers as Governor Leland Stanford drives the Golden Spike at Promontory Summit, Utah, to complete the transcontinental railroad on May 10, 1869. More than one thousand people, including immigrant laborers, gathered to witness the joining of the Pacific and Union tracks, which provided the United States with coast-to-coast transportation and communication."

Reporters in the nineteenth century often lived their stories and then wrote about them. Some, such as Nellie Bly, went undercover to expose scandals and problems in American society. The Transcontinental Railroad was news, from the rumors of financial mismanagement to the challenges faced by workers.

This activity will allow you to report on the first transcontinental train trip.

❯ **Read articles written about train travel.** You can find some at this website.

LOC golden spike 🔍

❯ **Imagine that you are a reporter.** Your editor has assigned you to cover the first passenger train across the country.

❯ **Write an article** about your experiences as a passenger on the first train to the West Coast. Some questions to ask include the following.

✱ Who are your fellow passengers?

✱ What are their reasons for traveling by train?

✱ What are their impressions of the trip?

✱ What are some of the views you see out the window?

✱ Do you witness any exchanges with Native American people?

✱ What are some of the stops along the way like? Is there time to explore?

✱ Does anything exciting or dramatic happen along the way?

CONSIDER THIS: Reporters are always looking for a story. What are other possible stories that might be written about a transcontinental train trip?

MAPPING THE RAILROADS

The rapid expansion of the West required ways to settle, transport, and communicate with the West more quickly. People began exploring ways to do this with the telegraph and the Transcontinental Railroad. This activity will explore routes for the Transcontinental Railroad and the effects.

❭ **Imagine it's 1855.** You have just been given the assignment of coming up with a route for the first transcontinental railroad.

❭ **Research where railroads are already built.** A helpful resource is the railroads maps collection held by the Library of Congress.

LOC railroad maps 🔍

* What are the western boundaries of where the railroad traveled during this time period?

* Where are the major towns along these western boundaries?

* Where are the major depots on their routes?

❭ **Download a map of the United States.** Research and mark the following in the map.

* Existing train routes

* Geographical features in the western part of the country

* Settlements in the western part of the country

❭ **Create a route for a transcontinental railroad.**

* Identify the **terminus** and both ends of the new railroad.

* Determine how the railroad will cross any natural barriers, such as rivers and mountains.

❭ **Prepare a presentation** in which you are "selling" your route to government officials and railway executives.

CONSIDER THIS: Research the telegraph and its role in western expansion. Why was it important for people to be able to communicate across the country? Could the Transcontinental Railroad have been built if the telegraph didn't exist? Could the telegraph have expanded across the country without the Transcontinental Railroad?

WORDS TO KNOW

terminus: the end of a railroad line.

acquisition: something bought or gained.

adobe: sun-dried bricks made of clay that are often used in areas with little rainfall.

advocate: a person who speaks out in support of someone or something.

ally: a country that agrees to help and support another country.

annexation: to add a new territory or area to an original area.

asset: a useful or desirable thing.

axle: the shaft on which a pair of wheels rotates.

blacksmith: a person who uses heat to make iron objects, particularly horseshoes.

boom town: a town that has tremendous and quick growth.

botany: the study of plants.

boundary: a line that marks a limit of an area, such as land owned by a country.

buckskin: deer hide.

buffalo chips: the dried dung of buffalo, which burns easily.

caulk: to close openings to make something airtight or waterproof.

cede: to surrender something to another.

chafe: to make sore with rubbing.

cholera: an infectious disease with symptoms of vomiting, diarrhea, and cramping.

climate: the average weather patterns in an area during a long period of time.

colonist: a settler living in a new land.

colonize: to settle a new land.

commerce: the activity of buying, selling, and trading.

Congress: a group of people who represent the states and make laws for the country.

conservation: protection through the preventing of loss or injury.

Continental Divide: the imaginary line that separates river systems that flow to opposite sides of a continent.

crop: a plant grown for food and other uses.

depot: a place for the storage of large quantities of equipment or food.

derailment: when a train runs off the rails of a track.

desideratum: something that is needed or wanted.

disintegrate: to break down or decay.

Dutch oven: a cooking pot that can be used over an open fire.

economic: having to do with the resources and wealth of a country.

elevation: a measurement of height above sea level.

emigrant: a person who leaves one country or region to settle in another. Before Oregon and California were officially part of the United States, pioneers were called emigrants.

epidemic: a disease that hits large groups at the same time and spreads quickly.

exclusion law: a law that prevents or expels someone based on their race or another characteristic.

exempt: to be free from an obligation.

exile: banished from living in a certain place.

expedition: a trip taken by a group of people for a specific purpose, such as exploration, scientific research, or war.

extinction: when a species dies out and there are no more left in the world.

Federalist: member of a political party during the late 1700s and early 1800s that favored a strong central government.

fertile: land that is good for growing crops.

ford: to cross a river at a place where the water is shallow enough for wading.

frontier: the edge of what is settled.

frostbite: an injury from prolonged exposure to extreme cold.

game: wild animals hunted for sport or for food.

geographic: the physical features of an area.

Great Migration: the mass movement of people to the West in the nineteenth century.

gristmill: a mill for grinding grain.

gutta percha: a tough, rubber-like material from tropical trees.

half-breed: a term, now considered offensive, meaning the offspring of parents of different races.

heirloom: a family possession handed down from generation to generation.

homestead: a dwelling and the land that goes with it.

immigrant: a person who moves to a new country to settle there permanently.

GLOSSARY

immunization: exposing a person to a tiny dose of a disease to make the person resistant to it.

incentive: something that encourages action or effort.

industrialization: when there is a lot of manufacturing, with products made by machines in large factories.

Industrial Revolution: the name of the period of time that started in England in the late 1700s when people started using machines to make things in large factories.

inflation: a rise in prices that leads to getting less for your money than you once got.

interpreter: someone who translates from one language to another.

intrepid: adventurous.

irrigation: to provide water for crops through ditches, pipes, or other means.

Isthmus of Panama: a narrow strip of land between the Caribbean Sea and the Pacific Ocean in Central America.

jack-of-all trades: someone who is good at many different kinds of work.

keelboat: a shallow freight boat.

land deal: a contract to buy or trade for land.

landmark: an object in a landscape that can be seen from far away.

latitude: the position of a place measured in degrees north or south of the equator.

livelihood: a source of income.

longitude: the position of a place measured in degrees east or west from the Prime Meridian line.

lucrative: something that is profitable, that makes money.

manifest destiny: the belief that the United States had a mission to expand across North America.

migration: the movement of a large group of animals or people from one location to another.

mineral: naturally occurring solid found in rocks and in the ground. Rocks are made of minerals. Gold and diamonds are precious minerals.

mission: a church where missionaries live and work.

missionary: a person sent by a church to persuade others to join or practice a specific religion.

moderate: a reasonable or medium amount.

Monroe Doctrine: the principle that any intervention by another country in the politics of the Americas is a potentially hostile act against the United States.

natural resource: something from nature that people can use in some way, such as water, stone, and wood.

negotiate: to bargain or come to an agreement about something.

Oregon Trail: the route settlers used to travel from Missouri to the West Coast during the 1840s and 1850s.

overlander: a person who traveled over land to the western United States.

pandemic: an epidemic that happens over a large area, on more than one continent.

patriarch: the male leader of a family or group. A matriarch is the female leader.

pelt: the skin or fur of an animal.

persecution: to treat people cruelly or unfairly because of their membership in a social, racial, ethnic, or political group.

pioneer: one of the first to settle in a new land.

pirogue: a long, narrow canoe.

profits: the amount of money made after deducting expenses.

prospector: someone who explores an area for valuable natural resources, such as gold.

prosperity: financial success.

provisions: needed supplies, such as food.

purify: to make something clean and pure.

rapids: a part of a river where the current moves very fast.

ratify: to officially approve something.

rations: someone's share of food.

rebellion: an act of open or violent resistance.

recede: to become more distant or move away.

regulation: an official rule or law.

repeal: to officially do away with something.

reservation: land owned by the United States but set aside for Native American tribes. There are about 326 reservations in the United States.

revenue: income or earnings.

sabotage: to deliberately damage or destroy.

sagebrush: a shrub that grows in the desert.

scurvy: a disease caused by lack of Vitamin C, with symptoms of weakness and bleeding gums.

sod: a section of earth with growing grass and roots.

species: a group of living things that are closely related and can produce offspring.

specimen: a sample of something, such as plant material.

stalwart: strong and brave.

stamina: energy and strength to keep doing sometime for a period of time.

staples: food or other products used regularly.

steam engine: an engine that burns wood or coal to heat water and create steam. The steam generates power to run the engine.

survey: to determine the boundaries, position, and form of a section of land.

telegraph: a device for tapping out coded messages over wires using electrical signals.

terminus: the end of a railroad line.

terrain: land or ground and all of its physical features, such as hills, rocks, and water.

territorial: describing a large area of land in the United States, before statehood.

territory: an organized division of a country that is not yet admitted to the full rights of a state.

transcontinental: across an entire continent.

treaty: a formal agreement between two nations.

tributary: a stream or river that flows into a larger river.

undercarriage: the framework underneath a vehicle, such as a wagon

Western Hemisphere: the half of the earth that contains North and South America.

westward expansion: an event of mass migration to settle the American West.

wholesale: large quantities of an item bought cheaper in order to resell.

yoke: a wooden frame attached to the necks of work animals, such as oxen, to link them for towing or plowing.

zoology: the study of animals.

RESOURCES

BOOKS

Doeden, Matt. *The Oregon Trail: An Interactive History Adventure (You Choose: History)*. Mankato, MN: Capstone Press, 2013.

Gunderson, Jessica. *Your Life as a Pioneer on the Oregon Trail (The Way It Was)*. Mankato, MN: Picture Window Books, 2012.

Hester, Sallie. *Diary of Sallie Hester: A Covered Wagon Girl*. Mankato, MN: Capstone Press, 2014.

Kravitz, Danny. *Surviving the Journey: The Story of the Oregon Trail (Adventures on the American Frontier)*. Mankato, MN: Capstone Press, 2014.

MUSEUMS

Fort Dalles Museum and Anderson Homestead
fortdallesmuseum.org

National Historic Oregon Trail Interpretive Center
blm.gov/learn/interpretive-centers/national-historic-oregon-trail-interpretive-center

National Oregon/California Trail Center
oregontrailcenter.org

WEBSITES

National Park Service, Oregon National Historical Trail
nps.gov/oreg/index.htm

Paper Trail: A Guide to Overland Pioneer Names & Documents
paper-trail.org

PBS, *Lewis and Clark: The Journey of the Corps of Discovery*
pbs.org/lewisandclark

Sacagawea, Lemhi-Shoshone
sacajawea.idahostatesman.com

RESOURCES

ESSENTIAL QUESTIONS

Introduction: Why did people risk traveling on the Oregon Trail if it was so dangerous?

Chapter 1: Why was the Louisiana Purchase important to the citizens of the United States?

Chapter 2: What effect did the Lewis and Clark Expedition have on westward expansion?

Chapter 3: What had to happen before people could begin traveling the Oregon Trail?

Chapter 4: What were some of the necessities people needed when traveling west on the Oregon Trail?

Chapter 5: What was the effect of the Oregon Trail on Native American history?

Chapter 6: What are some ways the Transcontinental Railroad changed life in the United States?

QR CODE GLOSSARY

Page 5: archive.org/details/msdos_Oregon_Trail_The_1990

Page 5: loc.gov/teachers/classroommaterials/presentationsandactivities/presentations/timeline/expref/oregtral/crossing.html

Page 8: oregontrailcenter.org/TrailCenter/OregonTrailPaintings.htm

Page 19: tjrs.monticello.org/archive/search/all

Page 19: monticello.org/site/jefferson/spurious-quotations

Page 20: avalon.law.yale.edu/subject_menus/ntreaty.asp

Page 20: archives.gov

Page 21: avalon.law.yale.edu/19th_century/louis1.asp

Page 22: lib.utexas.edu/maps/histus.html

Page 24: ourdocuments.gov/doc.php?flash=true&doc=23&page=transcript

Page 28: lewis-clark.org/article/2977

Page 33: pbs.org/lewisandclark/archive/idx_jou.html

Page 42: pbs.org/lewisandclark/trailmap/index.html

Page 42: nps.gov/parkhistory/online_books/grte2/images/fig3-5.jpg

QR CODE GLOSSARY (CONTINUED)

Page 43: pbs.org/lewisandclark/inside/saca.html

Page 43: nps.gov/lecl/learn/historyculture/sacagawea.htm

Page 43: nebraskastudies.org/0400/frameset_reset.html?http://www.nebraskastudies.org/0400/stories/0401_0107.html

Page 43: lemhi-shoshone.com

Page 49: pbs.org/weta/thewest/resources/archives/two/whitman0.htm

Page 56: oregontrailcenter.org/HistoricalTrails/PioneersTalk.htm

Page 56: oregonpioneers.com/diaries.htm

Page 57: en.wikipedia.org/wiki/Join,_or_Die

Page 58: memory.loc.gov:8081/ammem/award98/nbhihtml/psbibdateindex.html

Page 59: chroniclingamerica.loc.gov

Page 93: pages.uoregon.edu/mjdennis/courses/hst469_donation.htm

Page 93: ourdocuments.gov/doc.php?flash=true&doc=31

Page 95: plainshumanities.unl.edu/encyclopedia/doc/egp.war.017

Page 95: octa-trails.org/articles/trading-post-forts

Page 96: pbs.org/indiancountry/history/boarding2.html

Page 99: nps.gov/oreg/planyourvisit/placestogo.htm

Page 106: gutenberg.org/files/3177/3177-h/3177-h.htm

Page 108: nytimes.com/interactive/2009/03/10/us/20090310-immigration-explorer.html?_r=0

Page 108: teacher.scholastic.com/activities/immigration/immigration_data

Page 108: paper-trail.org

Page 108: youtu.be/5pp5dx2Q5Gs

Page 109: loc.gov/rr/news/topics/goldenspike.html

Page 110: loc.gov/collections/railroad-maps-1828-to-1900/about-this-collection

INDEX